2020
THE
YEAR
OF THE
ASTERISK

2020

*

American
Essays

THE
YEAR
OF THE
ASTERISK

Edited by
Greg
Gerding

UNIVERSITY OF HELL PRESS | PORTLAND, OREGON

This book is published by University of Hell Press
www.universityofhellpress.com

© 2021 GREG GERDING

Book Design and Layout by JEREMY JOHN PARKER
www.jeremyjohnparker.com/design

Published in the United States of America

ISBN 978-1-938753-42-8

Dedicated to every contributor in this book
and everyone who supports them;

with love to my wife and son
who support me.

IF IT'S NOT LOVE, THEN IT'S THE BOMB
THAT WILL BRING US TOGETHER.

—The Smiths "Ask" *Louder Than Bombs*

DO YOU HEAR THAT THUNDER?
THAT'S THE SOUND OF STRENGTH IN NUMBERS.

—IDLES "Grounds" *Ultra Mono*

TABLE OF CONTENTS

SEPTEMBER 2020

This is the inner molting that becomes a careful person. This is the fear that you must feel before you really engender self-protection.

To look inward and reflect on yourself is complicated. It's recognizing what you have inherited, what you have ignored, and what parts you need to improve.

It turns out that my father's suicide wasn't the end of the world after all; the only end of the world is the actual end of the world.

Existing while Black in 2020 is living on an edge, knowing that any interaction, any moment, could become a matter of life or death.

All this imposed time at home set the table for some very real, come-to-Jesus meetings with myself.

OCTOBER 2020

NOVEMBER 2020

Every political, social, ecological, cultural, or economic flaw in our society has been thrust back upon us all at once, with a generous helping of bad luck slathered on top. We played ourselves; we laid so many mines and rigged so many booby traps that we ran out of safe places to stand. COVID nudged us just enough to stumble, and then everything just started blowing up.

My father left on their 25th wedding anniversary. It seemed especially cruel then, still does. Even before he disappeared, I felt compelled to fill a void in my mother I couldn't understand or identify and, after all this time, I find myself unable to resolve conflicting feelings.

I had to remember to start the car occasionally in the evening. I'd sit inside and it smelled clean and fresh like a rental car and the interior lights would cast their amber hue. The little dinging sound, which might have been mildly annoying before, was cozy and faintly exciting. I'd start the engine and remember that I was a person who used to go places.

As we shelter-in-place, the anthill becomes our cityscape, the only bustle of activity within miles of the house we have grown into never leaving.

soul crushing … heart expanding

We're all just trying to navigate and survive the conditions of these garbage times. what statement do you want to make about it?

That was a question I jotted down, mid-2020, a thought that I didn't want to forget, a feeling. I underlined "Article Idea" at the top. And then I left it. Some day after that, I added to it.

2020*
The Year of the Asterisk

Early on, for anyone paying attention, we knew that we were *in the shit* and it wasn't going to resolve anytime soon. I imagined how, in every history book, every record book, every business ledger, any statistic associated with 2020 would have an asterisk, signifying how disruptive the year was for everyone and every aspect of society.

At its center was a highly contagious airborne coronavirus disease (COVID-19) that spread rapidly around the world. I read up on the history of pandemics and their impact. I adjusted my mindset and figured I'd better settle in; it could be a while.

After that, I returned to my journal periodically, writing brief notes about what I was thinking or experiencing, knowing later they might spark something larger.

music teacher ⟶ video

My kid was in school, well, not *in* school, but rather alongside me doing school via his laptop while I was trying to do my own work. It was his music class. His music teacher was engaging the students online, streaming live from inside her home.

There she was, sitting on the floor of her living room with stuffed animals arranged all around her; on her couch, on her coffee table, all of them facing her like an audience, like a classroom. Her neuroses on full display. She was singing to them.

jogger ⟶ bright orange shoes

The jogger earned a mention just for the sheer audacity of choosing to wear neon orange running shoes, unsettling everyone else, to appease his own uneasiness.

I already had the utmost respect for teachers
I didn't need a coronavirus

As if we were being punished for not appreciating teachers enough, a bible-worthy contagion was conjured to remind us of their value.

dead mouse on path
dead bird on path

I filled days with long walks, for relief. I noticed things that made me pensive. A dead mouse at the edge of the path, I steered clear. I then saw it every day for the next few weeks, decomposing over time. Until, one day, there was nothing left. Not a trace.

Soon after, on a colder day, near that same spot, I became peripherally aware of a bird standing there. As I came closer, at the moment I expected the bird to fly away due to my proximity, it was stock still, defiant. Except, it wasn't. It had frozen dead standing there.

If I didn't understand the dead mouse, the dead bird made it clear.

testing & tracking / investigating cases of COVID-19

The sheer failure of the president and his administration to sufficiently respond to this crisis, choosing inaction and assuming a "let's wait and see" stance versus activating every resource and all the brainpower to address. It seemed so simple: JUST CARE.

things I became an expert at: cutting our hair, masks, social distancing

new languages learned: Roblox, emojis, GIFs

I shouldn't have had to become good at any of these, but now I'm learned.

Trump ⟶ tank parade
groom ⟶ worst song request, Eagles "Lyin' Eyes"

I kept returning to Trump's request for tanks and missile launchers at his inaugural parade and how, when the military told him no, it seemed like every decision he made in the four years that followed was a tantrum directly related to that rejection.

My imagination spun. I thought of Trump as some groom with no sense for optics, demanding that the DJ play the Eagles' "Lyin' Eyes" during the wedding, just because it's his favorite song, and the DJ's flat reply, "Absolutely not, no way in hell," and how the groom was so miffed he deliberately gave all the guests coronaviruses.

The Eagles and "Lyin' Eyes" were the two worst things I could come up with on the fly.

rebrand coronavirus ⟶ Trump Virus
gladiatorial, Americanized
unsatiated thirst for death
not killing exactly who we're hoping it would kill

Trump tried to call the coronavirus "Chinese," but the virus was only made lethal by his fecklessness. It deserves to bear his name and all the gold paint that comes with him.

It was later revealed that when the COVID numbers suggested it was devastating the areas of America that didn't vote for him, he decided to leave it, that the deaths were playing out in his favor. Like he could aim the disease and fire it like a weapon.

Except, he eventually got it too. Like an ironic joke. Like karma.

Masks PSA
you can still shout through a mask
I forget when I'm wearing a mask that I can
still be heard

While adjusting to life with masks, it took a while to realize I could still speak. It felt like that should be a public service announcement directed at unmasked folks shouting about not wearing masks, to show them that they can still shout *while* masked.

The Only Tool, A Gun (police reform)
when LEO are asked to respond to so many
different situations
and are only given a gun to resolve

The police are overstretched and overburdened with all of the things they are asked to deal with, situations they are ill-equipped to handle. And the worst among them are racists. And they're all given guns, the only tool they focus on sharpening.

bigly, red ballcap
empty platitudes

From Trump's ascendance to the presidency and during it, independent thinking and common sense bled out. The fans that elevated Trump, first as a reality TV personality and then as a figurehead, revealed how little autonomy they wished to assert in life.

Anyone engaged in critical thought and a path toward betterment can see right through lies and empty platitudes. As Trump rode that golden escalator down, before he even opened his mouth, I didn't believe him. When he announced his run and all the awful words spilled from his face, he confirmed that he is the worst.

And the word "bigly" is a tell, much like the red ballcap now, that tips the listener to the character of the speaker and their bloated sense of self. And anyone who declares their plan as "big" or "best" or "beautiful" doesn't have any plan; that their plan is no plan; they have zero plan.

that one family member

On August 4th, 2020, I shared an article from *The Atlantic* by Ed Yong called "How the Pandemic Defeated America" which stated, "... few countries have been as severely hit as the United States, which has just 4 percent of the world's population but a quarter of its confirmed COVID-19 cases and deaths. These numbers are estimates. The actual toll, though undoubtedly higher, is unknown, because the richest country in the world still lacks sufficient testing to accurately count its sick citizens."

A relative wrote to me: "Greg, I can tell you at least two instances I know of personally where friends of friends have died from a bad heart. On their death certificate however was recorded COVID. Why? Because they get tens of thousands of dollars for each COVID case and thousands more for a ventilator. That's just one person knowing of two cases of falsifying records for profit. You want to know *why* the U.S. has a high rate?"

I wrote him back, "I want to know why the U.S. has *any* rate."

George Carlin

During my daily walks, I kept passing a guy who looked like George Carlin. Early on, when I realized I'd be passing him regularly, I said "hi" or gave a wave or nodded, extending courtesy. No response. Instead, his eyes were always fixed on the same spot a few feet in front of him. Never wavered. Same gait. Same pace. Same dead stare.

He looked like Carlin, but he was the alternate universe, utterly defeated variant. The one who had been squeezed of every last joke and couldn't come up with one for 2020, so he retired and waited for death. I think that's why I hate this guy. George Carlin would have figured things out straightaway; this version simply rolled over and quit.

*the call is coming from inside the house
the image in the mirror is the enemy*

Like the best horror movies lunging straight for our throat, except not a movie and very actually indeed already has us gripped by the throat.

None of these notes that accumulated beneath "Article Idea" were expanded into anything more. It was all too much to consider. That was 2020. It was *too much*. It was *enough already*. It was all of the stressful things coming at once. My coping mechanism default setting tends to be laughter, but there was nothing funny about 2020.

Every day, it felt like there was something new, something worse. I love America, but there's the *idea* of America, which everyone adores, and then there's the *truth* of America, which is terrible. There is a vast gulf between.

I stay focused on one goal: advocating a better place for the future of our children. Every system, every institution in America—social, political, legal, educational, medical, cultural, corporate, religious—has been exposed.

We have the resources and the wealth to lead in every important category (equality, healthcare, welfare, education, literacy, peace, climate protection), instead of every senseless one (incarceration, racial and gender inequality, ignorance, gun violence, student and national debt, military spending, fast food, and plastic surgery).

There was one thing I learned while reading about pandemics that was promising: The Black Death plague between 1346 to 1353 gave birth to the Renaissance. It stimulated patronage of the arts, science, literature, and philosophy. It resulted in an explosion of cultural and intellectual creativity.

Our society underappreciates artists (not you, of course, you're reading this). There is little support, and even less for bohemian types. But we're resilient. If anyone is built for these times, it's those of us who know you only need instant noodles or whiskey to get by, and we don't flinch at returning to a life with no money and no paycheck coming.

Artists, and those who value them, know how to survive; we adapt, we progress. We have the perspective, the language, a knowledge of the land; we have the map *and* the keys. We can write the survival guide. We think from fresh angles. We have worth.

Then, it struck me. As an artist, my time and energy during 2020 had to be spent attempting something meaningful.

The only way past is through.

I turned the page and wrote "Book Idea" at the top of the next one. 2020 needed to be captured raw, by many, and reported from the middle of the fire. I settled on "essays" as the form and narrowed the focus to "American" because of the wretched alchemy of "COVID" combined with "Trump," and its tragic result.

Initially, I thought about connecting with people via phone or video and transcribing their experiences. Instead, I invited the 51 people in this book to contribute an essay, coming full circle and asking them the same question I started with.

We're all just trying to navigate and survive the conditions of these garbage times, what statement do you want to make about it?

E ssay invitations started going out mid-August with an end-of-September deadline. It was a tight timeline, but my gut was telling me that whatever people wanted to say was already in their mind. They just needed the impetus to put it to paper.

As I sent out more invites over the weeks that followed, I'd shift the deadlines accordingly. Twenty essays came in throughout September, seventeen in October, nine in November, five in December. This book is organized by the months in which essays filtered in.

It was unreasonable to push deadlines in 2020, so I didn't; everything could turn on a dime (and would) and you had to manage expectations (any and all). And so, everything came in as it was meant to, and as personal readiness would allow.

I envisioned an approximation of "wartime reporting" because that's what 2020 felt like. A nation torn. A nation on the brink. I wanted to capture that mood, the challenges, the upset, the raw emotions that everyone was feeling. It felt important to nab them that way, to record indelible reminders of the year that was.

It is worth noting that I purposefully tried to collect essays prior to November 3rd, Election Day. The outcome was uncertain but would be incredibly impactful: the result would either continue the path of worse, or it would change course for the better.

Fortunately, America voted for relief, a release from further tyranny, and a chance for recovery. The essays in chapters "November 2020" and

"December 2020" came in following that election result. This fact implies nothing, it's just notable.

The book opens with a timeline highlighting notable events throughout the year for reference and context. *2020* *The Year of the Asterisk* aims to connect us through our shared experience; every one of us was alone and therefore together.

BRIEF TIMELINE OF NOTABLE EVENTS*

*The numbers at the end of each month represent US coronavirus statistics.

JANUARY 2020

JANUARY 21 – CDC confirms first US coronavirus case.

JANUARY 22 – Trump on coronavirus: "We have it totally under control. It's one person coming in from China. It's going to be just fine."

JANUARY 31 – WHO issues global health emergency.

0 DEATHS | 1 INFECTED

FEBRUARY 2020

FEBRUARY 2 – Trump on coronavirus: "We pretty much shut it down coming in from China."

FEBRUARY 3 – US declares public health emergency.

FEBRUARY 23 – Ahmaud Arbery is murdered by three white men in Georgia while jogging.

FEBRUARY 24 – Harvey Weinstein convicted of rape and sexual assault.

FEBRUARY 25 – CDC announces COVID-19 is headed towards pandemic status.

FEBRUARY 27 – Trump on coronavirus: "It's going to disappear. One day, it's like a miracle, it will disappear."

1 DEATH | 68 INFECTED

MARCH 2020

MARCH 11 – WHO declares COVID-19 a pandemic.

MARCH 13 – Trump declares COVID-19 a national emergency.

MARCH 13 – Breonna Taylor is shot six times, murdered in her home by police during a no-knock warrant in Kentucky.

MARCH 16 – Most schools nationwide are closed by this date.

MARCH 26 – Senate passes Coronavirus Aid, Relief, and Economic Security (CARES) Act.

MARCH 30 – Trump on coronavirus: "Stay calm, it will go away. You know it – you know it is going away, and it will go away, and we're going to have a great victory."

5,215 DEATHS | 199,391 INFECTED

APRIL 2020

APRIL 3 – CDC recommends all citizens wear masks in public.

APRIL 20 – Texas Lieutenant Governor Dan Patrick: "... there are more important things than living" as a justification for reopening businesses despite COVID.

APRIL 23 – Trump on coronavirus: "I see the disinfectant that knocks it out in a minute, one minute. And is there a way we can do something like that by injection inside or almost a cleaning? As you see, it gets in the lungs, it does a tremendous number on the lungs, so it would be interesting to check that."

APRIL 23 – Trump on coronavirus: "So, supposing we hit the body with a tremendous, whether its ultraviolet or just very powerful light, and I think you said, that hasn't been checked but you're gonna test it. And then I said, supposing it brought the light inside the body? Which you can either do either through the skin or some other way ..."

APRIL 29 – Trump on coronavirus: "It's gonna go away, this is going to go away."

APRIL 30 – Armed protesters enter Michigan's State Capitol building to demand an end to lockdown measures.

65,416 DEATHS | 1,118,284 INFECTED

MAY 2020

MAY 12 – Death toll "likely higher," Dr. Fauci testifies before a Senate committee.

MAY 19 – Trump on coronavirus: "When we have a lot of cases, I don't look at that as a bad thing, I look at that as, in a certain respect, as being a good thing … Because it means our testing is much better. I view it as a badge of honor, really, it's a badge of honor."

MAY 22 – Over 38,000,000 jobless claims have been filed.

MAY 25 – George Floyd murdered by police officer Derek Chauvin after kneeling on his neck for 8 minutes and 46 seconds in Minnesota, three other officers stand by and watch.

MAY 28 – US COVID-19 deaths pass 100,000.

MAY 29 – Trump on coronavirus: "We will be today terminating our relationship with the World Health Organization [WHO]."

MAY 29 – In response to George Floyd protests following his murder, Trump tweets, "… when the looting starts, the shooting starts."

MAY 31 – Further in response to the wave of civil unrest across the country, Trump says he will designate the far-left activist group Antifa a terrorist organization.

109,452 DEATHS | 1,877,717 INFECTED

JUNE 2020

JUNE 1 – Trump threatens to deploy the military to quell the riots, and then clears the streets between the White House and St. John's Episcopal Church for a photo-op.

JUNE 5 – During press remarks in the Rose Garden about improving jobs numbers and "equal justice under the law," Trump invoked George Floyd: "Hopefully George is looking down right now and saying, 'This is a great thing that's happening for our country.' This is a great day for him. It's a great day for everybody. This is a great day for everybody. This is a great, great day in terms of equality."

JUNE 5 – Washington, D.C. mayor Muriel Bowser designates a two-block section of 16th Street NW as "Black Lives Matter Plaza."

JUNE 10 – US COVID-19 cases surpass 2,000,000.

JUNE 12 – Rayshard Brooks is murdered by a police officer in the parking lot of a fast-food restaurant in Georgia.

JUNE 20 – Trump on coronavirus: "Testing is a double-edged sword .... When you do testing to that extent, you're going to find more people, you're going to find more cases, so I said to my people, 'Slow the testing down, please.'"

JUNE 23 – Trump repeats: "Cases are going up in the US because we are testing far more than any other country, and ever expanding. With smaller testing we would show fewer cases!"

130,879 DEATHS | 2,764,478 INFECTED

JULY 2020

JULY 7 – US surpasses 3,000,000 infections.

JULY 11 – Trump seen publicly wearing a face mask for the first time.

JULY 14 – Early Moderna data point to vaccine candidate's efficacy.

JULY 14 – Trump administration orders hospitals to bypass the CDC and send all COVID-19 patient data to a central database in Washington, D.C.

JULY 16 – US reports new record of COVID-19 cases: 75,600 in a single day.

JULY 19 – Trump on coronavirus: "Many of those cases are young people that would heal in a day. They have the sniffles, and we put it down as a test."

JULY 28 – Trump referring to Dr. Fauci: "He's got this high approval rating. So why don't I have a high approval rating with respect – and the administration – with respect to the virus?"

JULY 30 – Trump suggests delaying the 2020 presidential election, saying increased voting by mail could lead to fraud and inaccurate results.

157,887 DEATHS | 4,787,672 INFECTED

AUGUST 2020

AUGUST 3 – Trump on coronavirus: "They are dying. That's true. And you – it is what it is."

AUGUST 6 – Facebook founder Mark Zuckerberg reaches a net worth exceeding $100 billion, becoming the third centibillionaire, alongside Jeff Bezos and Bill Gates.

AUGUST 11 – Democratic presidential candidate Joe Biden names Senator Kamala Harris as his vice-presidential nominee.

AUGUST 16 – Due to a record-breaking heatwave and lightning strikes, hundreds of wildfires ignite across California.

AUGUST 17 – COVID-19 now the third-leading cause of death in the US.

AUGUST 23 – Jacob Blake is shot in the back in his car by police in Wisconsin, his three boys are sitting in the backseat. As a result, Blake is paralyzed from the waist down.

AUGUST 25 – Kyle Rittenhouse, age 17, kills two people and wounds another during protests against police brutality in Wisconsin.

AUGUST 26 – Amazon CEO Jeff Bezos becomes the first person in history to have a net worth exceeding $200 billion.

AUGUST 28 – First known case of COVID-19 reinfection reported in the US.

AUGUST 31 – Trump on coronavirus: "We've done a great job in COVID, but we don't get the credit."

AUGUST – Wildfires burn more than 8.2 million acres in American West.

188,692 DEATHS | 6,316,262 INFECTED

SEPTEMBER 2020

SEPTEMBER 10 – Trump on coronavirus: "This is nobody's fault but China."

SEPTEMBER 10 – Over ten percent of Oregon's state population flee from raging wildfires.

SEPTEMBER 14 – Pfizer, BioNTech expand Phase 3 vaccine trial.

SEPTEMBER 18 – Supreme Court Justice Ruth Bader Ginsburg dies.

SEPTEMBER 21 – Johnson & Johnson begins Phase 3 vaccine trial.

SEPTEMBER 23 – A new, more contagious strain of COVID-19 is discovered.

SEPTEMBER 23 – Trump on coronavirus: "I think we're rounding the turn very much."

SEPTEMBER 29 – The first 2020 presidential debate between President Donald Trump and former Vice President Joe Biden takes place in Cleveland, Ohio.

212,731 DEATHS | 7,543,766 INFECTED

BRENDAN CANTY

Making my bed over and over on the couch, and then folding up the blankets in the morning, putting them back on the black metal dog crate before anyone woke up. Madge barking once sometime between 5:30 and 7:00, an alert that she was older now too. Fifteen, about as old as dogs get, pretty deaf and blind, but possibly neither, she was being polite in her demands really. She needed to flush her system. She needed water. She needed more water these days, lots more. *Were her kidneys failing?* She got a lot of love from people who thought she was a puppy. A fact that we all found funny and mentioned to each other at dinner in a way to say that what did we know about how old a dog could get? If anyone felt safe enough to come over and actually pet Madge, they would see she had golden old-lady hair, thinning all over, that would never need a haircut again. She also had lumps that the vet, who since March would see her in the backyard, said were nothing we would do anything about anyway, noting her age. *I guess we are there*, I would remind myself. Madge's sister, Midge, had died two weeks previous, and the vet put her down in their front yard. She lived two blocks away. Fifteen years ago, I brought them both up from a pound in Lexington. Madge threw up in the car on the way home. Midge ate it. I took Madge. Best choice I ever made. The vet's kid is doing well in Hollywood. Prodigy of some sort, working on the remake of *Blazing Saddles*, animated, mixed with *Seven Samurai*, as a musical. The words seemed superfluous and stupid. *Where would you ever show a movie like that anyway? Who would take their kid to a theater?* The first business to disappear in our neighborhood, the canary in a coal mine, was the Uptown Theater. The biggest and most beautiful theater in the city, shuttered almost immediately. We all protested and promised to save our cinema, until we realized we had bigger problems. To this day, I wonder how AMC theaters knew so early that things were going to be this bad. I guess the big money has their own analysts. It's pretty easy to be peacefully walking around while knowing nothing. The process of becoming aware, educated, and then proactive, finally attaining conviction, takes time. Finally ridiculing the inconvenience initially felt and denouncing it in others. Nothing prepares you for living through something where you have so little control. The facts that we had gathered were, in a way, working against us in the early stages of this pandemic. Our son Leo, living in Chinatown in New York, came home. There was a lot of worry about being in close quarters with people, so instead of having him drive in his friend's car back to D.C., Michelle bought him a ticket on the train. We think that's where he got it. He and his friends traveled in a pack for a week or so. His one friend Cale, nervously standing away from the pack, went home pretty quick to Chicago. Leo got chills, we denied it. Leo coughed, we denied it. My oldest boy insisting that Leo had it. Then, he lost his sense of taste on the same day the *Times* wrote that that was a tell. So, we got him tested and put him in his room. Michelle is a nurse, so she was able to get him one of the hundred tests that her clinic was given, and she also took one for herself. Everyone in the city was becoming terrified. So many people were sick but unable to get tests. Everyone blamed the president, and our horribly incompetent and expensive medical system. We pay $1,600 per month. How could we fall so far behind the rest of the world that this was acceptable? We all had time to ruminate during the time it took to get their tests back. Ten days. She was negative, he was positive. So, she could go back to work. People weren't wearing masks yet, in part because no one had them. That was the other big outrage in the medical world, the PPE. Michelle was given one N95 mask a week. But they didn't always wear them, and in such a small clinic when her coworker showed up coughing one day and running a fever of 104 degrees the next day, Michelle got tested again and immediately sent home. This time the test came back in two days. "It's a new test," she says. *Thank god.* She self-quarantines. Mabel weeps from the hallway and wants to hug her mom. This time, Michelle tests positive. *Shit*. We mask up to bring her food, gloves too. She learns breathing lessons from a doctor on YouTube. Inhale, count to ten, repeat five times, exhale, cough. She sleeps on her stomach. She is taking this seriously. She is obviously worried, proactive. I am worried. She is taking medicine. CoQ10, melatonin, vitamin D. I take them too. Blood is becoming a worry. Our friend who died from a blood clot last month? Probably COVID. The two teachers at our school? That was COVID too. I would later lose two other friends to this, but back then the blood stuff was only starting. My heart was palpitating, I felt like shit. I went to the cardio doctor twice. He said I was fine. I had been sleeping on the couch. This is the inner molting that becomes a careful person. This is the fear that you must feel before you really engender self-protection. Sleeping, or not sleeping, on the couch wasn't helping anything, but our house was full. Asa had come home from Texas. Truett had been home since Christmas. Mabel turned 13 in April. Leo was home and hadn't left his room in two weeks. Michelle was in our room quarantined. And my nephew Sam, another refugee from New York, was living in our laundry room and watching the flights back home to Arizona with a mix of wonder. $59 dollars. Another bellwether. The end of something. Everything. I'm glad I got my touring in. I guess that's all over too. The venues. My booking agent said Paradigm laid off 100 agents by email. Big ones. Terrible times. Every night, I have plenty of time to worry on the couch. The profound despair and helplessness beget a terror I have never known. This is love. I am sure of it. This is a love aged 33 years. Threatened. Existential. This is fear. We take care of each other. She sleeps on her stomach. More breathing. I do the breathing too. I walk the dog. I do the breathing while walking the dog. Listening to a podcast about the plague. Reading a book about the Soviet front of WWII. I am not looking for respite. I need information. One thing we don't have. No one knows anything. That much is clear. It's bad. It does a bunch of bad shit to your body. But no one knows anything. Michelle doesn't die. She is negative one day, and the giant shelf of worry spills its contents onto the ground. We garden, celebrate birthdays, and are home. We clean the corners of our house and make the living room into an office. We cook Ethiopian food, and better food every day. We burn through movies. My nephew makes it back to Arizona. Leo finds a bigger, better apartment in New York for less money. Asa tutors a kid in Bethesda. Mabel is in online school now, a secular hippie school in Vermont. This is the first time in 18 years we don't have anyone in D.C. public schools. But it's all a mess anyway. I feel like we haven't left the house in six months, except to shop and walk Madge on her route. In so many ways, she is still a puppy.

We got chickens, a bat flew into Asa's room in the basement, and Truett raised a catbird chick who had fallen into his window well. Feeding it wet cat food every day, protecting it from the cats. And finally, after teaching it to eat off the ground, it hopped on the boxwood, then the garage roof, and was suddenly gone.

ALEX DANG

"God, can you tell me how much longer I'll get to be alive and in love. God, I am sorry for the times I didn't want to stick around." —Hanif Abdurraqib

A nd if you're reading this, that means you've made it through to the other side of 2020. Friends, what a year it has been. I'm glad you're still here.

I think a lot of us thought 2020 was going to be "our year." I sure thought it was! I was coming out of 2019 with a breakup and randomly occurring seizures. I had left a job that I loved but wasn't cut out for. I kept running into wall after wall until I saw each obstacle was just me getting in my own way. I was ready for a new start. 2020 looked like the perfect place to begin.

Reader, when I ask you, where do you come from, do you think of a place or a people? Does it hold you like a childhood bedroom? Do you think of what you've done? Do you come from the wreckage of your mistakes? Are you from a family or a country? Would you defend your home? Have you ever had to protect your loved ones? Did someone you care for say, "See you tomorrow!" and when tomorrow came they had left? It seems like every day the world is ending and every day it keeps going and gets worse and better and then so much worse. But hasn't this always been the case?

When the wildfires began and Oregon burst into flames and the sky reddened and the smoke bellied the air, my dad said to me, "This reminds me of the day Saigon fell."

My mom nodded, "Just like the war."

People tell immigrants to "go back to where they came from" and I wonder if they know the reasons why you would run in the first place. There are a lot of things to run towards: opportunity for you and your family, a better, shinier life for your children. It's a matter of where you want to go and that's always a matter of perspective. But when it's a matter of life or death, you aren't running towards something. You're running away from something:

A death. A war. An ending.

And when America yells, "Go back to where you came from!" I want to ask, *Do you mean to the house your hands ransacked, or to the grave you robbed?* And when America demands us to be grateful for being here, I wonder if they have ever traced their lineage of blood and smolder back to the beginning. Do they know we are escaping a war they started? And America tells us how lucky we are for surviving.

2020 has left us gasping with questions. I am swallowed by the whys of it all. Why is this happening? Why didn't we listen? Why couldn't we have prevented it all? Stare through the window at the world falling apart or turn my gaze inside and only see myself, myself, myself? To look inward and reflect on yourself is complicated. It's recognizing what you have inherited, what you have ignored, and what parts you need to improve.

I see how extremely lucky and privileged I've been during all of this. The seizures are being treated and have been connected to my newly diagnosed bipolar depression. While figuring out my health situation, I've been staying with my parents (I'm writing this from my childhood bedroom!) and have had their continual support. There have been times when I had a seizure and my mom or dad was there to catch me before hitting the ground. This is not a metaphor. I am so incredibly grateful and oftentimes will think I am undeserving of this love and care. I keep asking, *Why me?* And every time my friends and family will gently hold out a hand so I won't fall. They remind me until I start believing it for myself.

In high school, I always felt like I was *too emotional* and isn't it funny how I am writing in the same room considering those same feelings from this newer me? I am so much closer to my family now. Those emotions 18-year-old me would have struggled to understand are now the same ones I tell my brothers about, the ones I ask my mom how to deal with, the ones my dad checks up on.

Oh, bless the younger versions of us, filled with truths and doubts; they who have so many reasons, but are all out of excuses.

The world caught on fire (again) and is still burning and it is hot even as the winter creeps in. When we look back at this year, what will we remember? America has looked within itself and what do we see? When the embers die out and the world is ash and soot, what will sprout from the ruins? Who will survive the flames?

Something new has grown inside of us. Reach into the earth of yourself and gather the harvest. What are you going to do with this bounty? Will you plant something for the next generation? What will you do with your hands? I have burst forth with anger and gratitude and sorrow and guilt and joy and anger and love and joy and joy. I have seen friends and doctors and artists harness their rage into tools to build a new world. There are students and mentors and strangers shaping their sadness and anger and love into shields and homes; into hammers and poems.

Friends, this was our year. And the next year will be ours too, and the year after that and the year after. It will always be our year to do something.

"Deep calls to deep
            at the thunder of your cataracts;
all your waves and your billows
            have gone over me."
—PSALM 42:7

"I'm on my way to the promised land."
            —AC/DC, "Highway to Hell"

In *Love Warrior*, author Glennon Doyle writes that "grief is love's souvenir," and I would add only that every souvenir of love is enjoyed alone.

The aloneness of the pandemic grief experience is a different kind of aloneness from the one I felt in the days immediately following my father's death. That aloneness felt entirely personal, a lonely aloneness that no one else had access to, only barely penetrable by those who had also lost a parent to suicide.

This new grief is a collective aloneness, encompassing the debts owed to the planet and its people by the death machinery of capitalism. This machinery played a part in my father's death as well.

Two years of grieving a parent is still early days as far as grief is concerned, and the added grief of a global pandemic is like a weighted blanket on top of another weighted blanket. It feels like suffocation. I don't remember feeling suffocated after my dad died. I felt other things. Desperate. Angry. Abandoned. Afraid that I would die the same way, alone in my house. The one sensation that does translate across the two experiences occurs every morning during the first few moments upon waking.

A liminal space that exists between sleep and consciousness, where all you're aware of is your presence within a body. You haven't quite registered where you are. Maybe you've noted the color of the room you're in, the sound of a wind chime outside, but you haven't yet *remembered*. And when you do, the visceral response is profound.

When my father died, that response was weeping. A turning on my side toward a wall or the corner of my mother's sofa, a sort of infantile retreat. During the pandemic, the response is anxiety. My heart rate quickens, my chest tightens, I can't breathe. This is my best evidence that what I am dealing with is not COVID-19 but severe anxiety regarding COVID-19, and I hold onto that evidence for the remainder of each day. *All you have to do is go to sleep, I tell myself. And when you wake up, you'll feel normal for a minute and you'll know you're not sick.*

Is there a word for this early morning grief liminality, like the hypnagogic jerk that jolts you out of sleep when you're just on the verge, but in the opposite direction? A jerking back into the space of brutal truth. A hypnabrutic truth jerk.

Thanks to the pandemic, I find out that I have a medical condition that can manifest as anxiety-triggered esophageal spasms that mimic the experience of a heart attack. I have four over the course of the first week of quarantine. I receive a medical exam in the parking lot of an Urgent Care while a lady in a minivan watches me from a few parking spots away, and I am prescribed strong anxiety medication that knocks me out for the rest of the day, but that evening I have the worst attack yet while in the middle of stirring a dinner pot. The nausea and lightheadedness, the feeling that my life is on the brink of cessation.

I immediately turn off the stove burner and lie down on the tiled floor, breathing deeply in through my nose and out through pursed lips. My heart rate continues to increase. I get up and walk to my bedroom where I collapse in bed and proceed to have rigors, the word the doctors used to describe my convulsions in the hospital years ago when I went into septic shock after kidney surgery. I wait until my legs stop convulsing and go to the bathroom. I turn on the shower, take off all my clothes, and kneel in the bathtub beneath the hot water. My heart rate slows after about ten minutes, whether from the hot water or the passage of time I am not sure, and I dry off, get dressed again, lie back down in bed, and call my mom.

The fear of going to the hospital at this time is intense. Instead of putting myself and other people at risk, I speak to a cardiologist via a friend who works in the department and determine that my risk of heart disease is incredibly low and that the likeliest culprit is GERD (gastroesophageal reflux disease). I am given advice on how to manage my symptoms, and especially my anxiety, and I follow them for the next six months with no recurrence of attacks. I now know that the esophagus and heart are similarly enervated such that pain in one results in pain in the other. What feels like my chest threatening to bust me wide open is what is known as a "nutcracker" or "jackhammer" esophagus embroiled in a violent spasm of anxiety it has never felt before.

The pandemic grief experience is shared on social media, in Zoom meetings, on phone calls, while watching the news. And despite the collective nature of it, the disparities between different classes of people have never been more apparent, the chasm of opportunity and access laid bare. The masked restaurant servers carrying plates of food to the maskless paying guests. Those who deserve protection and those who serve the protected.

It turns out that my father's suicide wasn't the end of the world after all; the only end of the world is the actual end of the world.

Two years before my father's death, he calls me high on opiates and whiskey and tells me, "You and I are spiraling down into an abyss together and I don't know how to stop it." The sentiment terrifies me because of my lifelong fear that I am identical to him, that his darkness is my darkness, that his abyss might be mine as well.

A year after his death, a friend teaches me how to use I Ching, a divination method my father used for years after picking up the habit on his many business trips to China. The first and most pressing question I can think to ask is, "What do I need to know about my relationship with my father?" and the hexagram I receive is #29, The Abyss/Danger, which informs me that the real danger of the abyss is in the fear of it, the fear of loss of self in the shadow of my father that has haunted me since childhood, that the darkness of such shadows is relative. I can't help but wonder if he received the same hexagram three years before, if he assuaged the shock of it with substances and was still so overcome with fear for me that he made the call as a warning.

In my final phone call with my father, he admits regret that he'd ever thought Trump would be "not so bad" as a president.

"I lived through Nixon," he'd said when I called him in panic the day after the election, "and I can't imagine him being any worse than that."

At the time of our last call, two years into Trump's presidency, he says that he now thinks Trump will cause the end of the world.

The way everyone lives now is the way my father lived every day for years. Having a virulent and highly contagious disease meant that he had to sterilize everything in his home if he wanted visitors. He had two bathrooms and never used the one intended for guests out of fear of infecting them. To this day, a particular combination of Clorox and air freshener brings me right back to my father's apartment in the days after his death. I smelled it once while staying in an Airbnb in Santa Fe, then again at the Albuquerque Sunport. Even a particular brand of scented trash can liners I purchased once reminded me of my father. Every time I opened the door to the cupboard beneath the sink, I was back in Detroit.

In the early days, before I had been quarantined in isolation for so long that sterilizing everything no longer mattered, every time I used a Clorox wipe on a door handle or a drawer pull, I thought of my dad. I know that he felt contaminated in a way that was inescapable, and that he feared contaminating others. I also know that that fear extended beyond mere medical concerns.

Is my father's abyss a personal metaphor for my time in quarantine, or is the quarantine itself a metaphor for my relationship with my father? Am I overthinking all of this in my aloneness?

In 2005, when I'm 22 and haven't spoken to my father in four years, my 31-year-old husband and I take a ferry across the Irish Sea as we move back to Dublin from Leeds, where we've spent two years living alone together for the first time. We're going back to Ireland to care for his great aunt who has developed dementia; he is intent on preventing her admittance to a retirement facility. The ferry crosses the sea at night and is filled with plush seating and a small cinema for passengers to watch movies during the voyage. Thinking myself superior, I step out on deck instead to enjoy the air and look out across the waves. My husband and I approach the rail and I lean forward to get a good look. What I see frightens me: nothing. The sea is invisible in this darkness, replaced with a vast void identical to the cosmos that hover above it. *I feel existential*, I find myself thinking, as if juxtaposed against this eternal emptiness my inconsequential existence is thrown into stark relief. As if I could fall into those waters and disappear and the world would go on, indifferent. It's the first time I can remember truly understanding the meaning of the word abyss. Intent not to stare long into it, I cross my arms to warm myself and turn away from my husband who remains on deck, undisturbed by the proximity of the end of the universe. I enter the common room of the ferry, seat myself in the cinema with a handful of strangers, and watch *Legally Blonde* until the ferry docks.

A friend tells me, in response to my esophageal attacks, that I am a "canary in the coal mine" who understands the enormity of an event before most people. I don't think I'm particularly psychic, but I do read voraciously. I want to receive my information from epidemiologists, not politicians, and I spend the first weeks reading as many reports and predictions as I can stomach until I find out from the most authoritative sources that we're going to be in this for at least eighteen months. It will take at least that long to create an effective vaccine. At the same time, everyone around me claims society will return to normal in April. A friend asks me when my partner and I plan to throw our next party and laughs when I say, "Not until at least 2021," only to text me months later to admit that I'd been right.

I learn to forgive people for their denial. Many of us have been brainwashed and propagandized beyond the point of sanity, led to believe that the road to salvation is a pile of cash behind door number two and that fascism is wielded by those who name themselves after its opposition. We want to believe we won't get sick, that no one we love will get sick, that our lives won't be forever altered, scarred.

Watch the pastor tell his congregation that God is larger than this "dreaded virus," that he himself is stronger than it because he speaks to God, and when that pastor dies watch his daughter tell the world, "it becomes very real to you"

when you see the ones you love die from disease.

I find myself grateful that my father chose his own exit.

Two years after my father's death, and right at the start of the pandemic, the ravens visit my yard. They usually hang out in a barren tree owned by my neighbors across the dirt road, but the neighbors have taken to shouting at the birds to "fuck off!" and they are seeking refuge on my fence posts. One day while I sit on the front porch reading a book, I hear the first raven issue a low cronk noise to its buddies across the way, as if to signal a new safe haven. At first, I'm not sure if it's a raven or a crow, but its size gives me a clue and I spend the afternoon listening to YouTube recordings of crow and raven calls, learning to discern the differences. Their beaks are also distinct, ravens having a subtle hooked curve at the tips of theirs.

I read more about ravens and find out that their symbolism includes an ability to mend broken timelines, to carry space from one moment in time to another in order to heal a wound. I think back to the day my father left Taos and I knew then somehow that I would never see him again, how I've always considered that an instance of time "folding in on itself" where I received a glimpse of the future as it was laid over the present. Did the ravens visit me then, too, and what wound did they heal with this action?

An entire abyss placed inside a raven. What rifts in time are you mending now, and do we get a choice?

Before the pandemic, I had this strange fantasy that my life was being devoured by some otherworldly creature, like Stephen King's Langoliers or the Reapers in *Doctor Who*. I'm trapped inside a church in a damaged timeline while flying gargoyles devour people on the road outside, all the other buildings, until slowly, eventually, they attack the oldest structure in the area with all its new and fragile people inside. I can't help but watch as those around me are consumed by menders of time. I have felt for two years that I must be next. The experts call this survivor guilt. When the pandemic arrived, first came the panic that I had been right, the fear that my fantasy had been another insight from the ravens. Six months in and I've come to realize that what many of us have labeled anxiety and paranoia are sometimes the realm of those who pay attention. And in a pandemic, survivor guilt is compounded in those privileged enough to be a witness instead of a victim, at least for now. Guilt in all its self-absorbed glory, fully knowing it can do nothing but watch and wring its hands on Twitter while the world burns.

I have become Justine in *Melancholia*, dismissed as neurotic and fragile in the beginning of the film only to have her mysterious, doom-laden fantasies proven accurate by the time the world is subsumed by another planet. My father and I saw the movie together at the West End Cinema in Washington, D.C., as part of a holiday film-hopping extravaganza. He visited me for Christmas and we spent three whole days going from film to film, theater to theater, until we saw most of what was playing at the time. Months later, my father called me to ask, "What was your favorite film of last year?" We both chose *Melancholia*.

He said, "I had a feeling you'd agree with me. I don't know why, but I can't stop thinking about it."

The story of grief over the death of a father is the story of grief over a lost way of living and loving in this burning world. I'm interested in recording the nebulous, the not-defined, the space between gone and now. How to paint a portrait of someone who has left the room. How to accept that, after this, nothing will ever go back to whatever we thought was normal.

Somehow, the collapse of society is simultaneously a sudden shock and far slower than we ever imagined, both instantaneous and agonizing in its pace. The was/is line has a certain date, but the timestamp is less clear and the moment stretches interminably until it breaks.

While in a Zoom call with fellow writers, we sit in silence typing away at our own manuscripts in an attempt to mimic the lost cafe experience, and a delivery driver pulls up to my house blasting "Highway to Hell." The FedEx tracking website told me I'd need to sign for these packages, but these days we do no-contact delivery. I mute my audio on the Zoom call to avoid distracting anyone with this interruption, open the door, and wave to the driver who wears one blue nitrile glove.

"I figured you were home," he tells me. "So, I signed for you. Have a great day!"

"Thanks, you too!" I call after him, and "Highway to Hell" bears him cheerily off into the distance.

HOPE AND HELPLESSNESS: EXISTING WHILE BLACK IN 2020

ASHLEY JAMES

March 2020 shocked the world. It felt like in one moment I was living my best life—attending sporting events, bar hopping, planning a spring break—and in the next cities shut down, people were sick and unemployed, and the leaders of our nation politicized a virus. Like many people, I started to experience anxiety, sleeplessness, lack of motivation, and a feeling of impending doom.

One thing that kept me sane during the early stages of the pandemic was walking in my neighborhood. I had recently moved to Atlanta, Georgia, to start a master's program, and rented a room in an upper-class neighborhood called Morningside-Lenox. Though I almost never saw another Black person on my walks, I enjoyed this neighborhood because of its overall liberal feel. Many of my neighbors have "Black Lives Matter" signage or other messages expressing allyship. This is a stark contrast to where I grew up in Virginia, where my neighbors fly confederate flags and lawns are littered with "Trump 2020" and "blue lives matter" signs.

Two months into quarantine, I decided to break my isolation and meet a friend for a socially distanced walk in the park. The thought of driving to meet a person in real life excited me! I pulled out of my parking spot, queued up the most recent Megan Thee Stallion song, and headed out of my cul de sac, the happiest I had felt in weeks. After driving only a few feet, I was briefly blinded by the setting sun, and within seconds heard screams and saw frantic waving arms around my car. I pumped my brakes and a few seconds later, after I had fully stopped, a red-faced white man slammed his fists into my windshield with such force that it split the entire thing into a million cracks.

I jumped out of my car to see what happened and the red-faced man screamed, "You almost hit my fucking daughter!"

I was horrified. Horrified at the thought that I almost hit a child, but also frightened that the group of white parents supervising their children's play in the street now surrounded me, one of whom was so angry he smashed my windshield with his bare fists.

I apologized over and over, "Oh my God, I'm so, so sorry. The sun was in my eyes, I couldn't see. I would never hit a child, I'm so sorry."

The parents around me kept saying, "It's okay, everyone is safe, it's okay." They seemed to be trying to defuse the entire situation.

Obviously, my mood was ruined, so I just returned to my car, made a K turn, and drove about fifty feet back home.

When I pulled up, my roommate and landlord, a conservative middle-aged white woman, was sitting on a lawn chair reading. I can't say I processed this at the moment, but in retrospect, I knew her identity as an upper-class white lawyer would warrant a respect from the man who smashed my windshield that he clearly did not have for me. Given that I don't fit the demographic of the other residents on my street, he probably believed I did not belong there. I felt that my landlord could provide proof I lived in the neighborhood, protect me from any possible further assault, and help to ask the man to pay for the repair, which as a graduate student, unemployed due to the pandemic, I could not afford to replace myself.

I explained the situation to my landlord and, though hesitant at first, she agreed to walk with me to the scene of the incident. The only people left at the scene were a woman and her husband. My landlord asked the man if he was the one who smashed my windshield.

Clearly offended, he began verbally attacking me, said that I was speeding and on my phone (neither of which were true), and then in a threatening tone he said, "Do you want us to call the police? Because we could!"

At that point, his wife interrupted him. She said the man who smashed my windshield was her friend who lived on another street, and she felt uncomfortable disclosing his identity.

"You have to understand," she said, "it was a gut reaction because you almost hit his *daughter*."

My landlord and I explained that we really just wanted the man's contact information to discuss payment for the damage. However, she stood her ground and ended up taking my information instead. The next day, the woman sent me money on Venmo to replace my windshield, claiming that her friend would pay her back.

The more time passed, the more I realized how traumatic that situation was. For the first two days after, I cried violently. For the next few weeks, I replayed the scene in my head—waving arms, smashed windshield, expletives. My feelings morphed from terror to anger. I would tell myself, *Even if he thought I almost hit his daughter, it wasn't okay to smash my windshield. Would it have been okay if he hit me? I'd ask myself how I could have done things differently. Should I have called the police? My neighbor seemed to think he should call the police* **on me**. *Was he threatening my life? What would have happened if I spoke up in the moment? Would the neighbors support me? Would I learn the identity of this angry man, who I might encounter again?*

As months passed, these thoughts lessened, but even now I often cruise down the Atlanta roads and then suddenly visualize a red face and fists crashing into my windshield.

This incident represents what 2020 has become as a whole for me. America has witnessed multiple accounts of white violence against Black people—Ahmaud Abery, Breonna Taylor, George Floyd, Jacob Blake, Rayshard Brooks. Like my neighbor defended her friend by saying, "It was a gut reaction," people defend those acts of violence, saying, "He was resisting arrest," or "They had a warrant."

The day after the incident, I met the windshield replacement technician outside my home, and at least three of my neighbors asked if I was okay, expressing that they witnessed everything and were disgusted at the man who smashed my windshield. While I appreciated the concern, I wondered why they said nothing when it happened. Similarly, people witness the murder of Black people nationwide and remain silent.

However, there are also people, like my landlord, who speak out and stand up. I was surprised when she came to my door the night of the incident, hugged me, and said that she did not think the man would have smashed the windshield if it were *her* in the car instead of me. I have also been amazed and inspired by the protests, boycotts, and marches in response to the killings of Black people in 2020. Police have brutalized people of all races night after night, and yet the protests continue.

As a Black woman, I have long been aware of how deeply racism is ingrained in every aspect of American society. However, in recent years, I feel like racism has been so ubiquitous that I've become numb. I've tried to block out the reality of so much hate in this world with pretty neighborhoods and "Black Lives Matter" signs on lawns. 2020 taught me that isn't possible. For like Richard Wright wrote in regard to lynching and white brutality, I also only needed to hear about the aforementioned killings "to feel their full effects in the deepest layers of my consciousness."

2020 has been an emotional rollercoaster of shock, grief, anger, despair, hope, and helplessness. Existing while Black in 2020 is living on an edge, knowing that any interaction, any moment, could become a matter of life or death. Trump has tried to suppress the nation's attempts to acknowledge racism in the U.S., characterizing systemic racism as a "twisted web of lies." But I know it would be a disservice to myself and my country if I didn't constantly read, write, and act to dismantle our corrupt and unjust systems.

As long as I am breathing, I will not be silent.

LIZ SCOTT

March is when 2020 started for me. End of March is when my good friend and I decided to postpone our annual joint birthday get-together, a cherished tradition where we'd pick one new fancy restaurant each year, toast each other with champagne cocktails, and gripe about getting older. Better safe than sorry, we'd wait a few weeks and reschedule. Same with my weekly bridge game. We canceled on the last Sunday of March hoping we could resume the following week. I've got to cop to feeling annoyed with what was then the recommendation to self-quarantine for a couple of weeks, but fine, okay, I can do that. Whatever.

Then, April. It took a minute but everyone I knew yielded—even if less than willingly—to the reality. Weeks, maybe even a couple of months. For the first week or so, I groused. I complained and felt put-upon. And then—gradually and unexpectedly—I could feel something else begin to germinate. Everywhere you'd hear, "We're all in this together," and what had once been a glib, throw-away line was now a felt reality. John Lennon sang on my Spotify and the lyrics were no longer an abstraction. I watched videos of animals all over the world freely roaming in places they probably hadn't for centuries; saw images of vistas across the planet of striking blue skies, free from smog and pollution. The birds were singing louder, the bears were returning to Yellowstone, and the skies were blue in New Delhi. In such a short time—and in supreme irony spurred by a pandemic—our planet had started to heal.

And here's what some of you might find, shall we say, weird. I kept thinking about Joaquin Phoenix. (Don't judge!) During his speech at the Oscars in February he said, "I think we've become very disconnected from the natural world. Many of us are guilty of an egocentric worldview, and we believe that we're the center of the universe. We go into the natural world and we plunder it for its resources. We feel entitled to artificially inseminate a cow and steal her baby, even though her cries of anguish are unmistakable. Then we take her milk that's intended for her calf and we put it in our coffee and our cereal."

I was feeling my place in the natural world more intensely than I ever had before. And more connected too; connected to the planet we've been entrusted with, to my circle of friends, to my dear family, to my sweet cat, and to *all* my fellow creatures of earth.

And these other things: I welcomed the imposed solitude. Gone was the dilemma of figuring out how long I'd have to stay at some social event before I could excuse myself and go home. My basically introverted nature became undeniable. I've certainly taken time in my life to reflect and be still, but the mandate to stay put created a more uninterrupted ground for reflection, where before my days would be broken up by quick trips to the store or a walk with a friend or a movie. All this imposed time at home set the table for some very real, come-to-Jesus meetings with myself.

May. I Marie Kondo-ed my closet—filled bag after bag after bag with clothes I hadn't worn in decades and was keeping, *exactly why?* I organized my bureau drawers and my kitchen cabinets. I alphabetized my bookcase. I even attacked my museum of spices. And every single, solitary day I danced to a Zumba class on YouTube till I dripped with sweat, 45 minutes at least. Every. Damn. Day. I was on fire. Internal reflection gave way to a focus on more external things. I blew through to-do lists like nobody's business. I don't know when I've felt so organized and industrious.

And then there was May 25. Almost immediately after the murder of George Floyd, my blessedly progressive city answered the call and I joined the army of peaceful protesters that took to the streets. And in another experience of supreme irony, during the most isolated time of my life, I felt such a strong sense of connection and affiliation with the multiple millions of people around the globe who were marching too. It's probably too soon to know, but the pandemic has created the time, space, and opportunity to finally be resolute in our attention to the national shame that's only had piecemeal consideration up till now.

June. I have not worn pants with a zipper for over two months and I haven't used under-eye concealer, eye liner, or lipstick and you have to know that, before, I wouldn't even have walked the few steps to the trash chute with dark circles under my eyes because, who knows, someone might walk by. I have cut my own hair—with manicure scissors. I haven't exercised once. Not. One. Single. Time. And don't ask about showers! I have gone to seed. I have even less attention span than usual. With all this time, you'd think I'd make a dent in that stack of books on my bedside table. You'd think I'd write even a sentence in my new book project. You'd think I'd clean the laundry room and the closet in the guest room where I close my eyes and just pitch things in. You'd think I'd vacuum or do laundry. You'd think I'd cook or meditate or, or, or.

What I've done instead is read the Op-Eds in *The New York Times* and toggle between: Netflix, Hulu, Amazon Prime, Sundance Now, Quibi, Sling, Disney +, Acorn, Fubo, and Lexi (I made that last one up). It's that or MSNBC so I can scream along with like-minded folk.

July. Ditto.

August. The relentlessness of it all. In my old life, I had some anxiety, sure. But there were also trips to plan, holiday traditions, dinner parties, theater tickets.

Now the future is worry about the impact of this lost year(s) on my 12-year-old grandson. It's no trip to Africa that we'd been planning for three years. It's not being able to hug my friends. It's mounting terror about November 3rd and the aftermath with all its dreadful possibility. It's wondering if I will live long enough to see the end of this. That's the future.

September is here and I see no end in sight. The rest of 2020? Or 2021? Does anyone think it'll be any different? And as if to prove that, yes, things *can* get worse, the west coast is on fire. The air where I live has the worst air quality in the world right now and people are wearing gas masks to get their Starbucks. Only the cynics, the ignorant, and the obscenely greedy can deny the reality of how climate change is ravaging our planet.

I feel my resilience dissolving. I do have a new dog and I am already deeply attached to him. I cherish my family. I know I am so much more fortunate than many. But I can't imagine when I'll ever wear that black dress I bought in February. I can't imagine going to Ava Gene's restaurant, with tables packed together, people free to sit closely and laugh loudly. Or to the movies. Or to a reading at Powell's where I'd be sitting next to friends I'd greeted with a hug. I can't imagine planning a trip—to anywhere! I'm glad to fully own my basic introverted nature, but I also crave the liveliness of my old life. What about that?

Where I find peace these days is to pull the lens way, way out; to remember my smallness in this universe and consider this all as a reset. In my work as a psychologist, I see all the time that we almost never make changes unless we *have* to, when our self-destructive behavior catches up with us. Change is just too fucking hard. So far, our planet has managed to rejuvenate in the more than four billion years of wars and pandemics and the rages of nature. Maybe the destruction that we humans have inflicted on our planet is finally catching up with us. About time.

I don't know how or when, but my dearest hope is that I will integrate the sense of connection and affinity that I felt in April. I will do my best to frame this as a season of rest and rejuvenation on every level; to breathe deeply and think deeply; to accept that reset is no longer optional—not for me, not for this country, not for the human race, not for the planet.

May it be so.

E very day brings something else, doesn't it? That is probably the thing that makes so many people uncomfortable now. Speaking to you from the middle of 2020, it feels like the worst part of all of this is that you never know what's coming next.

Not that you ever know what's coming next anyway. This is the basis of all great television—there is always the possibility that, right now, things you have never even considered are aligning to wait until just the right moment to fuck up your momentum. It's tiring. We just want to know what's coming towards us. We just want to say, "It's okay, we have a plan for this."

This year, most days, most people I know sit around contemplating the latest reminder of how short, nasty, and brutish life can be without any hint of irony. If you aren't doing that and you aren't pretending your core is a quivering jello salad of anxiety, then you may be somewhere far outside the year 2020— and, please, let it be the future. It feels obvious that the future might exist, but this year has been profoundly unsettling. So many sure things have been taken from us—industries, traditions, connections, institutions.

Last week, wildfire smoke made the air so polluted here that breathing it made you sick. In my house, we all stayed in one room with the windows and doors taped around the gaps. We put a filter on the back of our fan and played card games in our tiny square of manufactured air. *What science fiction*, it felt like, *to need to make a contraption to make breathable air*, but it was no fiction.

It just never ends. The cycle of *surprising event*, and *reaction*, and *reaction to reaction*, and *surprising event*, lays out a Möbius strip that no one is even trying to step away from. It is so hard to pull your brain from the fight-or-flight you feel in the face of history's pen. Unsurprisingly, stress levels are up across the country. And, in true stereotypical style, people still want to label certain joys as juvenile or saccharine. You would think people would take any reason to be happy or proud lately, but instead my friends send selfies with deep bags under their eyes. They don't make art. They don't write. They don't accept compliments. Whether it is work stress or lack of work stress, whether we are alone or apart, there is always some reason to deny yourself something that makes you happy.

2020 has destroyed any plans I had. It destroyed the plans I had to make plans. It is overwhelming. It feels awful to feel awful and not be able to set up a ladder to get yourself to feeling better. This is what I was thinking on a walk a few months ago. I was lonely, but I also desperately needed to be out of the house and away from the people I lived with. My college commencement had been canceled. My graduation had been pushed back a term anyway. I wasn't sure who would hire me in an economy like this. And, that day, a new report had come out about murder hornets. When held together as one burden, it all felt like too much. For the first time in many years, I didn't know how to fix what was wrong. I didn't even know what fixes would be available, or if other breaks would occur.

Around me, flowers bloomed and bees buzzed. These are things I normally delight in. Scratch that—these are things I am fixated on. I have lost friends because I send them too many pictures of my seedlings. There is something so magical to me about the way plants grow. A date palm found in Israel germinated after approximately 2,000 years. How can there not be a metaphor for patience in the way seeds will wait, and wait, and wait, and still go on to grow?

And how awful would it be to sit waiting all that time and not enjoy the world around you? Don't tell the blue sky that it's not enough for you. Is it not amazing the way some rocks will sit in the same place for centuries before they shift? What do you gain by ignoring these wonders of your world?

I'm getting through 2020 the same way I get through every other year, one day at a time. I still don't really know how to fix the things that are wrong on a large scale, but I'm finding ways to fix things around the house. Maybe I thought this would be the year I could see weeks and weeks ahead, but maybe when you're looking weeks and weeks ahead (or weeks and weeks behind), you miss the world around you, and the things you love that are still happening, right now. 2020 feels like it has taken so much away from everyone, but there's still joy here, and I refuse to turn it away.

Every day, I sing a thank you to my house plants for ignoring the upheaval. I kiss my husband's face and tell him he is the best person I know. I pet my cat's stomach and feel grateful when he purrs. I feel grateful when instead he strikes, too. If there is a day on the horizon where I do not get to wake up to his claws gently kneading the back of my knee, then I refuse to let the gloom of the year steal away these days where we are both here. I know what grief looks like when it's been refracted through the lens of regret; it's how my mother's face reflects onto my heart.

So, I let the bad news come. It was always going to anyway. Trying to pretend the bad news doesn't exist is, to some extent, how 2020 got to feeling so out of control. Not being able to plan for the future is still no reason to throw away the present. Every day, my plan is now—deal with the shit and, when it's dealt with, don't forget to look around for the small pleasures that are still here. Treat yourself to a walk. Stop and smell a rose. The air is clear now. It wasn't before, but it is now, and don't you love the perfume of flowers? It's the kind of thing that gets you through a winter. These small pleasures, they're the kinds of things that make it worth living through 2020.

Portland, Oregon. *Illahee, on the Willamette River.*
September 7, 2020, 7:33 p.m.

This season, there's a bad mix of wildfire and wind. And, with what I've learned from the last three months of protesting injustice, here's exactly how some folks would fix this situation we're in now due to a lack of adequate forest management or even a shared definition of what fire is in our society:

1. If you just ignore it, you won't give it any energy. You'll deprive the fire of the attention it's seeking, and it will go away.

2. Your vote is important! Vote in an anti-fire President and Congress in November. Then, we can begin to finally fix the air quality and the constant ash clouding East Multnomah and Clackamas Counties when we have the right representation.

3. Like Crow with Red Wings when he captured the sun. Here we are unfolding the heat we all held within. You cannot hold fire in one hand, ash in another, and say we are not all related.

4. Let's all start fires of our own! Let's reclaim the fire and show the fire that it's not the only fire that can *be* a fire. So, let's all show up to the fire with fire of our own, we can even make songs about the fire to show the fire how creative and resilient we are when it's literally burning our houses down (again). Or we

do that ourselves to show it who's boss! Let's burn down *our* house—or, even better, the houses of our neighbors of color as an act of solidarity—to prove that the fire can't really hurt us!

5. Let's try to reason with the fire and really see what side it's on. You know, those fires are from rural areas and they just don't understand our city way of living, like the high cost of housing or making the world practically unbreathable due to Portland's totally incessant and unnecessary use of cars in a 20-mile area when there are streets literally built to do the same job as a fire. I mean, highway. Whatever. Let's talk to the fire so it sees how much we value discourse and its point of view, and maybe it won't burn us. Next!

6. Actual Nazis are driving around unsupervised in Downtown Portland and Salem right now and in the past few days the Portland Police Bureau tear-gassed an entire neighborhood and beat down a black man in the Lents neighborhood outside of the Portland Pickles Baseball Stadium in Lents Park. Lents Park is where I take my child to practice baseball because it's one of the few things we connect on. The Portland Police tear-gassed the Lents neighborhood to the point that black children could not breathe in their own homes, did this knowingly to make the neighborhood unsafe and turn citizens against Anti-White Supremacist demonstrators. And, today, we couldn't go to Lents Park, where children play on play structures specifically designed for sensory and autism spectrum individuals to touch and have feedback made just for them for once in their lives, and now it's as toxic as the society that says that if it doesn't like you, you don't deserve anything designed for you, it will smoke you out and make you run.

7. I told my family today that I'm ready to leave the country. It was breakfast, or lunch. It was breakfast. It was lunch. It was before the winds came and I had to tell my child to go inside because it's not safe for a child here.

8. Tell me again, tell me how waiting until the fire passes and I can breathe again is going to solve this. Tell me how touching the fire, how caressing it like

a child, a lover, a familiar, how letting it engulf my body until it consumes me as I am one with it, tell me that my embers will become change as I blaze with it through the streets of my own city, as I watch from within it destroy the bodies and lives of children, the life I have with my own child, the life, the lives, the life, the lives, this this this this ...

It's been more than 100 days since George Floyd died at the hands of white supremacist Minneapolis Police. But I'm asthmatic. And I choke easily on everything that's trying to kill me. Like the ash. And the wind.

And the smoke.

And the fire.

RAN WALKER

When we were little, kids would run around and hit us on our birthdays: the number of times that matched our age, plus one to grow on. As we grew up, we always kept an eye out for that extra lick, that "one to grow on."

What we didn't understand back then was that, by the time our birthdays came around, we had completed the year of that age and were now entering a new year, like when you celebrate a child's first birthday and they'd been experiencing year one since birth. That "one to grow on" was a way of christening our body for the year we were growing into.

In 2019, the city of Hampton, Virginia, where I have resided with my family for thirteen years, celebrated the 400 years that had passed since the first Africans were brought to Hampton (formerly called Point Comfort) on the Portuguese ship *White Lion* in August of 1619. *The New York Times* published a collection of articles and essays, initiating what is now commonly known as *The 1619 Project*.

When I reflect over what all of this means for my family and me, it begs the question: How much has the experience of being Black in America changed since 1619? Well, if one takes into account the explosion of protests in 2020 and the rush for corporate America to make the saying "Black Lives Matter" something stylish to say while unarmed Black men and women continue to still have their deaths relegated to hashtags with no prosecution (and, often, no indictments) of their murders, I'm left to feel like America has not evolved all that much since the original policing of Black bodies began over 400 years ago.

For most people, 2020 probably started off as a regular year, before a sudden shitstorm broke loose with COVID-19 and the Black Lives Matter protests. America was cooking all along, though. It's just that the temperature was being raised so slowly that many people didn't notice that things were about to boil. Pretty soon, all of our arrogance and hate would be on full display for all to see—but this time it wouldn't just be the voices of Americans raised, it would be voices from all over the world. It would be clear that we were in the midst of not one pandemic, but two; and like the quest to find a COVID-19 vaccine, we are finding ourselves in the quest to find a vaccine for racism, sexism, homophobia, transphobia, xenophobia, and all of the other social ills that have arrested the evolution of our country.

But, in spite of all of this, I remain optimistic that change will come; that we will continue to evolve for the better, one day at a time. We lived through yesterday and we are living through today and, if given a chance, we will live through tomorrow. Although our memories might appear short, a glance at history shows that this country has been through great, even devastating, challenges and managed to bounce back.

When Black Americans celebrated 400 years of survival in this country back in 2019, we took the 400 licks that came along with each year, but 2020 reminded us that we still had "one to grow on." That "one" was a huge blow, but in the classic Persian adage, "This, too, shall pass." We will continue to fight to make this country reach its full potential and, with a little luck, we can use 2020 as a catalyst to make that happen.

My friend Donna was outside my front door, calling up from below. I had shut the screen door, to let in the late summer breeze, leaving the solid door ajar. I couldn't see her, and she couldn't see me, but I knew she was there because I'd heard the door to her floating home open and close, its distinct sound, and footsteps, a few quick ones and then nothing.

She knew I was home because of the screen. I always close the main door, always lock up when I'm not there. She knows these things about me. We had traveled together, to Hawai'i, back in January, when people from the mainland could go to the islands without quarantining for two weeks. A lifetime ago.

"So, I see you're halfway out with the Black Lives Matter thing!" she teased, her alto voice wafting up the stairs and into the second-floor kitchen, where I was making chef salad since it was too hot to turn on the oven. I figured all of B row could hear. My mouth tightened in that uncomfortable way it sometimes does, and my lips formed an unrehearsed retort.

"I'm not halfway out about *anything*!" I shouted back. "You of all people should know *that*!"

Immediately, I felt my face flush, felt a guilty twinge. Guilt for reacting to my next-door neighbor in so abrupt a way, and guilt that she had my number. My new Black Lives Matter yard sign, given to me by my daughter, was indeed partially obscured by a variegated hosta and an English boxwood, planted in colorful ceramic pots on my front deck. The sign leaned precariously against the blue metal siding of my house, ready to be carried away by a strong wind, the buffeting kind that occasionally overtake our little utopia west of Portland.

When you live on a marina, it's the only option you have, container gardening. There is no grass. There are no yards or flower beds.

About the sign. I could resist the notion all I wanted, but truth be told, I was halfway *in*. And, as Donna had dryly observed, halfway out, too. Our waterborne community along the Columbia River is wonderfully diverse, a generally peaceful place with nature trails and abundant wildlife nearby. Hardly anyone ever yells, unless someone falls into the river, and then they haul them out. In our neck of the woods, comprised of live-aboard boats and homes perched on Lincoln Log-style foundations of crisscrossed timber and giant, old-growth logs, we've got Boomers and Millennials and Gen-Xers, retired folks and folks still working, nurses and steel fabricators and jewelry makers and preschool teachers and emergency responders, rural renegades who are done with the suburbs, perhaps for good.

On B and C rows alone, there's a lawyer, a library director, a restauranteur, an animation specialist, and a death doula. People help each other, sharing their time and their tools, food from their pantries, and the occasional handwritten note. "Thinking of you," say some cards left on doorsteps. Or "happy birthday" or "congratulations" or "feel better soon." The winter of 2016, when it snowed for a week straight, my neighbor Bill grabbed a ladder and a wide shovel and got up on my roof, removing a foot of white stuff to make sure the house didn't capsize.

"I don't want anything," Bill said when I inquired about paying him. "Make me a pan of lasagna sometime."

I did, that very week.

This has been the weirdest summer in the five years I've lived here. Not because of the pandemic, per se, though it has presented a unique challenge for people who have to walk up two docks and two ramps just to get to the parking lot, invariably passing others along the way. There's no such thing as 100 percent social isolation in a community as geographically dense as ours, even if you order your groceries online and have them delivered. Eventually, you have to come out of your house and, when you do, someone will be out on the docks.

We have folks who wear masks all the time and others who hardly ever do, folks who fear COVID-19 and folks who think it's overblown. Our Dutch friends, who always come for "the season" between June and October and make us all feel more cosmopolitan, stayed put in The Netherlands this year because of travel restrictions related to the virus. It's been odd and somewhat disquieting to see their big boat, *Talmar*, stay tethered in its slip, all buttoned up, its white window blinds shut, no happy-hour gatherings on the main deck, no fun-loving laughter amplified across the water.

As the rhetoric has heated up over three months of racial-justice protests in the next big city over and at police-support events here in town, I've noticed the tone at the marina shift slightly, too, with signs showing up outside homes hinting at their occupants' ideological leanings. American flags fly from sailboat masts and Thin Blue Line flags flutter from the upper decks of homes. A pair of This We Believe signs—bursting with neon colors celebrating marriage equality, women's rights, immigrant rights, the rights of people of color, and the right of the planet to, well, exist—showed up after the Fourth of July.

And then there's my Black Lives Matter sign, peeking coyly out from behind a spray of foliage and the reddish head of a metal-sculpted heron, an attempt to say something—anything—that might help lift up an entire demographic whose members have never enjoyed full access to everything the Land of the Free is supposed to offer; life, liberty, and the pursuit of happiness, for starters.

A certain cognitive dissonance plays inside my head, like a well-worn cassette tape, tinny and garbled in places, threatening to snap and unravel at any moment. I want to say my piece. I want to keep the peace. I'm a middle child, terribly allergic to conflict. Why can't we all just get along?

I spend too much time wondering if we'll be able to surmount the intransigence that defines this moment in our history, when we've taken sides and, in some cases, taken up arms to defend the existential point of view that most strongly resonates for each of us.

I really want to be part of the solution, not the problem, moving forward into fall. The tape keeps playing, low and insistent.

I go outside, water my plants, pick off some of the dead bits. I stare at my sign, think about taking it down. I turn around, see a woman across the way wave at me from C row. She coils up her hose, flashes the peace sign, smiles.

The wind shifts. I leave my sign alone.

BRIAN S. ELLIS

t is fall 2019. I get home from work and my wife is finishing up having tea with a woman we're both friends with. She's a bit older than us and lives in the neighborhood. I say hello, but don't talk much, as I'm often still carrying the stress from work and am not ready to interact. I work with young children and always come home covered in snot, spit, and sometimes urine. I go into another room to change. The woman says her goodbyes and then my wife comes back to our bedroom. When she opens the door, she's blinking like she does when she's trying to remember the name of an actor.

"How was tea?" I ask her.

She sniffs and re-focuses her eyes.

"Good," she says, in a tone that means not so good. "There was this tense moment right at the end there," she pauses to sigh, "I always forget Margaret is an anti-vaxxer."

We know Margaret from what can loosely be described as a plant medicine community. Tea rooms, cacao ceremonies, sound baths, and the like. It's all very stereotypical Portland, all very woo. I haven't always been like this. I am from New England originally, and there will always be that black wool brass buckle part of me, but a decade into living on the west coast and my latent paganism has come to full bloom. In my house there are candles, essential oils, altars. We closely follow the phases of the Moon, use the constellations like Rorschach tests, ritually imbibe spirits.

It's March 2020. COVID-19 is here. Lockdown has begun and I am no longer working. The whole world has moved their socializing onto the internet and I see on Facebook that Margaret is posting about masks. About *how dangerous they are*. About *how they restrict oxygen*. About *how they don't work very well*. And *anyway, the virus is not as bad as they say*.

In the intervening months, my wife has engaged with Margaret about her anti-vax leanings, in the non-confrontational, calling-in way. In these interactions Margaret is willing to concede some points, including the most vile lies about the connection between vaccines and autism, but she retains a vague uneasiness about vaccines, claims that the body is better at healing itself on its own. And so we thought progress was being made on Margaret, a few more hard conversations and we could bring her back into the fold; that perhaps this is due to her age, the targeted disinformation pushed by YouTube and/or Facebook, but also maybe this is just the unintended problem of being an open person— being too open to the good has let some of the bad in.

Then came COVID and Margaret's mask posts. She wasn't the only one, another friend, Jeremy, a father and musician from the same circle of people as Margaret has been posting videos online. He doesn't give a full-throated endorsement of the videos per se, just mentions that they bring up some interesting points ... even uses the ellipsis like that, a punctuation mark I've always loathed, as replacement for providing evidence. These videos contain conspiracy theories about vaccines, 5th generation cell phone towers, and Bill Gates. It was all couched in vagueness, using the language of non-confrontation and the ellipsis as tactic to spread dangerous lies. It was then that I started to feel like we're losing people, that my open and free thinking woo-woo friends had been pulled so far around the ouroboros that they had been sucked into the same conspiracies held by the fascist right.

Conspirituality as a term has been around since 2011, coined by Charlotte Ward in the *Journal of Contemporary Religion*. More recently, writers Julian Walker, Derek Beres, and Matthew Remski started a podcast to discuss the overlap of conspiracy theory and spirituality. But I like the way another writer, Jules Evans, put it, which I'm paraphrasing here: the inverse of the ecstatic *we're all connected* is the paranoid *it's all connected*. Through this lens, those that are spiritual, particularly those outside major religions, would seem particularly susceptible to conspiracy thinking. But I don't know if this effect is that narrow or new. In Eugene Taylor's excellent book *Shadow Culture*, he traces outsider spirituality all the way back to the Shakers and the Ephrata Mystics. Reading *Shadow Culture* in turn inspired me to read *When Prophecy Fails* by Leon Festinger et al., the case study that first brought us the theory of cognitive dissonance. The authors of the case study infiltrated a group called The Brotherhood of the Seven Rays, led by a woman named Dorothy Martin. Dorothy received messages via automatic writing from a planet called Clarion, where Jesus had been reincarnated as the alien Sandana. Dorothy Martin's belief system hews closely to that of the Pleiadeans, who have some overlap with QAnon, that vaguely assembled wad of conspiracies that includes but is not limited to: Alien DNA, mind control nanochips, Lizard People, and a fictional drug invented by Hunter S. Thompson that supposedly is being harvested from children.

As I've sat with this, the people in my community who have gone from spiritual free thinkers to QAnon conspiracy theorists, are not people who have gone so far to the left that they have ended up on the right. The difficult realization that has come to me is that these worlds have always had a wide overlap, and the way that they are all connected is in white supremacy. Part of the diabolical machine of whiteness involves the ways that it is hollow, a concept and identity constructed to support oppression. It seems natural for those of us who are white to go looking for another culture, desperate to find something of substance, and in doing so colonizing and appropriating whatever culture we try to take on. In this way, the whiteness is not escaped, but further strengthened. My people, the black wool and brass buckle folks, went looking for a life of more spiritual substance and, in turn, decided to set into motion a genocide. Not much has changed. This is the real conspiracy, except it is not a conspiracy because it is out in the open. There is no part of this culture that it doesn't touch. There is an important question about access. Part of the reason other cultures are made available to be consumed is white supremacy and its sub-genres colonialism, imperialism, and capitalism. Yoga studios that push out

Black businesses on Albina Avenue and Alberta Street and Mississippi Avenue here in Portland are easy to find fault with. Harder is interrogating your own spiritual connection to the land, of naming oneself a Wicca or Druid, knowing that this land belongs to the Chinook. That last sentence was addressed directly to myself. This is the work I need to be doing.

It is early July 2020. There have been protests in the streets of Portland every night for a little over a month. And when I am out in the street, I am filled with a surprising amount of hope, that the oppression of the police is finally being confronted, after decades of violence at the hands of the state being a non-issue. The hope I feel being in a crowd chanting for justice evaporates when I come home and see how the protests are being reflected in the media. On Facebook, Margaret is posting about rioters and looters destroying our city. An attitude that, I suppose, was predictable. But something I used to see as an arc, the radicalization of people by YouTube and Facebook and Fox News, I now see as weakness that has always been there. The crucible of 2020 has caused a lot of new suffering, but it has also illuminated things that have been with us since the beginning. This year, 2020, has discovered ways to exploit every weakness that was baked into this culture. This year has brought into vivid detail all the work that needs to be done. Societal and structural work is a big part of it, but the interpersonal, personal, and even spiritual are part of it as well. There is so much work I need to do, in my community and with myself, to interrogate my presence in this place and, if possible, find a way to help bring a greater measure of justice to this land. It's all connected.

DIAN GREENWOOD

A ugust 31, 2020. COVID-19. Month five. Over 183,000 deaths and 6,000,000 cases. Two political conventions, virtually. My eldest granddaughter contracted COVID-19 while she and her roommates partied away their disappointment after the expectations for their college graduation celebrations had to be abandoned. Black Lives Matter rallies continue nightly in downtown Portland. People are justly angry. Others lament, "We want everything back the way it was," supported by the ongoing question on the lips of every near-hysterical newscaster, "When will this end?"

So, today, I'm channeling Frida Kahlo, complete with similarly dangly earrings like the ones Trotsky gave her, the white hands hanging down near her shoulders, along with the brilliant red/orange/gold many-stranded necklace made by a Guatemalan woman under the hot equatorial sun, most likely while sitting on a mat in front of her hut. What would Frida do inside COVID-19 and the Black Lives Matter movement while fires and hurricanes and tornadoes race across our broad country and our national leaders wage war among themselves, fighting like tiny tots on a playground over who gets to own the drum? In many ways, our mostly progressive and powerful country doesn't seem to know who we are anymore or who we're about to become.

We've previously succumbed to smallpox and diphtheria, scarlet fever and polio. Now, COVID-19. What if the pandemics never end? If not this virus, then the next one. Remember Ebola? H1N1? Would we finally stop waiting for the way things were before COVID-19? Would those who are able plan long-awaited vacations and delayed family reunions? (Some have already risked them.) Would I look forward to traveling the seven minutes to my therapy office, recently boarded up and now in a fight for its life? Or prefer my comfy chair at home and the new Zoom culture?

What would Frida do? She would march at the front of the protest on Southwest Third Avenue. Walk arm in arm with leaders of Black Lives Matter, her hand-embroidered turquoise mask, the embroidered flowers swirling in arcs, a butterfly at the center. She would stand in front of the microphone, her small and broken body lifting her braided hair wrapped into a crown and laced with flowers and brightly woven cloth. She would be there in a wheelchair if necessary. Her fist would be in the air. Her fierce voice would rise with passion into the microphone. She would yell, "Down with oppression! Power to the people!" She would be the first to throw the flame onto the waiting rubbish to burn a larger-than-life Trump effigy. She would not turn back until the police retreated.

Instead, channeling Pema Chödrön, the American Buddhist nun, feels truer to my nature. In her case, the crowd would need to be very still to hear her voice. "Make *this* moment count," she would say. "Change is inevitable. The tsunami of disruption we're living through is part of the change." She would recommend sitting quietly and doing *tonglen* ... first, breathing in your pain, then your friend's pain, after which you breathe in the pain of your enemy ... yes, your enemy. Finally, "Breathe in the pain of the world. The whole world. Breathe in the pain on the inbreath, breathe out peace on the outbreath." Like Martin Luther King, Jr., she would recommend non-violence. "Take a giant step back and ponder: how am I at war with my sisters and brothers? With myself?" Ask, "How can I bring peace into the world?" Finally, "Breathe."

A younger, more energetic me did *not* join the protesters in San Francisco and Berkeley's People's Park during the sixties and seventies. What I did was sit on the floor with my husband and listen to Chicano leaders in the Mission prepare for the farm protests. I led young kids from the Western Addition in a dance contest, dancing my ass off to get their shy selves to join me. Taught Poetry in the schools in Bernal Heights before it was a trendy neighborhood. Prepared sandwiches for my young son before he boarded a bus to Hunters Point during the effort to desegregate the schools. Led consciousness-raising groups for middle-class wives in Marin County. A different version of my mentors, Frida Kahlo and Pema Chödrön.

Here's what I know: we're in the middle of COVID-19. I'm seventy-eight years old. It's time to let go. Not give up, but let go. To finish the books I've worked on for almost thirty years that say what I need to say. To welcome my hair's natural transition to gray. Walk a mile or two a day just to keep my body from turning in on itself. I'm letting go of my too-abundant library. Of people who overreact or live too long on the surface of things. As a therapist, I get paid to witness and grapple with those responses. I wear skirts because they're cooler. Forget makeup. In the evening, while the network news blasts into living rooms, I take a friend's novel down to the outside deck and read before dinner and PBS News. I write contribution checks, post candidate signs in my window.

Sometimes, I'm lonely. But my small raised-bed garden gives me more pleasure than I could have imagined. Others who find this time productive join me in looking beyond the devastation of COVID-19. I wash my hands, wear a mask. Vote. Through *tonglen*, I hold close the heartfelt demonstrators who raise placards like Frida would. Wrap my arms around the fires ravaging our forests and heartland, the devastating tunnels of wind decimating our coastal cities and seaboard states, embrace the hungering poor and the many faces of those who have died ... yes ... hold them inside my meditation. Like Pema would.

If I sound selfish, I am. If I have a pre-existing condition, I do. I miss getting in the car and driving to Seattle to see family. Flying to San Diego to see a son is out of the question. But what I have is a beautiful place to live, enough food, and meaningful work. I'm privileged. I remember that fact every day.

When I take Frida "inside" and down into the golden cave where all things churn and transform inside me, I take her passion and use it to enhance the one primary tool I have: my voice. When I invite Pema to join us, I use her calm and freedom from expectations to mold that passion and allow it to simmer and stew until it's ready to walk up the stairs and out of the cavern into the world. Knowing I am not Frida. Knowing I am not Pema. I am who I am. My voice. These words the tangible, concrete artifact I have to give.

TRAVIS LAURENCE NAUGHT

YouTube has gone from "a friend I call a few times a year" to "a roommate." Our relationship has matured. It started out as a fling, fumbling around together when no one else was answering. Now? I wake up and check to make sure I haven't missed anything.

It's a business arrangement, actually. This office has always had its door open for me, but it wasn't until mid-April 2020 that I went through it with a worker's mindset. Hours and hours of learning material are waiting for the motivated employee. A word to the wise, though: not all classes contain strategies worthy of adding to your personal playbook. Some of the clowns offering advice have forgotten their floppy shoes and red noses at home.

Besides, carpooling is *so* 2019.

There's not a profession or hobby that is not covered ad nauseum in the video catalog available. For crying out loud, hundreds of people have posted clips of themselves opening shoes! And those segments have been viewed by millions. I try not to judge. You want to show off some flashy new kicks and the outside world is too scary for you to do it in public? Throw up the video and let that public come to you. Brilliant.

I've been an in-person convention salesman for years. Not shoes, though. Comic books and collectibles are my jam. Dragging stuff out of storage and letting others walk away with it if the price is right. Not to brag, but I was rather good at convincing an awful lot of people that the price was right. One guy in 2011 didn't even know he wanted to buy a hockey jersey before walking by me. It looked good on him as he walked away.

The first show I was scheduled to sell at in 2020 was Gem State Comic

Con. Actors from the *Star Wars* and *Land Before Time* franchises, artists from DC and Marvel, and other special guests were going to draw thousands of people. The proximity of excited individuals competing with one another to walk out with the comeliest of loot would create a frenzy of cash exchanging hands and eventually leave dealers feeling like the shellshocked citizens of Aleppo left to piece together the remnants of their city after the most recent attack.

Sorry. That was insensitive. I should have gone with the metaphor of a worn-out stud horse after a day with the stimulus rod. Nope, that's not any better. It's difficult being all "woke." I mean, guilty feeling. I mean, aware that my actions affect others. I mean, I'm so grateful that today I am more cognizant of the way my words land, while at the same time respecting my previous self for being so open with the world about the internal mechanics of dealing with surviving on a day-to-day basis.

What the hell just happened?! I was lamenting the fact that societal circumstances kept me from reveling in a good day's hard (though exhausting) work and my conscience chimed in. *Shut the fuck up, cricket, I'm being selfish here!*

Gem State Comic Con canceled a month prior to their scheduled date. It wasn't heartbreaking, by any means. By the time the news broke, the proverbial writing had been on the wall for several days. College basketball tournaments had already been canceled. Major league sports had closed for an indeterminate amount of time. Bars were bulging at the seams with crowds clamoring to get their last drink in before being told that somebody in a state-level office cared about them and they had to get the hell out; and, yes, that meant home.

It was time to learn a new technique. YouTube's homepage offered suggestions based on my previous (somewhat illicit) searches while the cursor blinked in the search bar. My first step was basic. I stated out loud, "This is going to be my job."

I searched "collecting comics." A mind-boggling number of hits were retrieved. Five or six down, I recognized one of the creators as a dealer from whom I purchase monthly mystery boxes. Seemed as good a place to start as any. I dove in.

Now, I watch fifteen hours of content per week. Most of those hours revolve around listening to folks speculate on the future of an uneven industry.

It is a microcosm of the larger world. No company intent on growing beyond a few miles' radius isn't figuring out how to capitalize on the web, to connect beyond their local community. And what's wild is that even local communities have been shuttered to our availability. Not only is it easier to click the button and order something today, but it's also safer.

No, it's not my favorite. Hell, I went to a butcher shop today just to get out of the house. I spent less than four minutes inside the store, mask on, with only one other customer. It was all I could do not to race over to them and ask for a hug. Seriously, missing connection with other people is REAL. I was able to resist that urge, come home, sanitize myself and my meat sticks, and pontificate my behavior of the last few months.

History will remember my time in 2020 because I uploaded a smattering of my own videos. Mine are not high-quality. High-definition, sure, but poorly produced with the most basic software. Mine are nowhere near the level of masterpieces produced by Comic Tom and Very Gary (the two individuals whom I watch most). Mine show me, a middle-aged man in a wheelchair, watching my dad open boxes of graded comics for fun and to be a part of some larger community, since I can't be a part of the community in my own backyard right now.

Full transparency: I did post a shoe unboxing video. My young niece and nephew helped me open the pair of custom Chuck Taylor's I ordered during one of my bored moments early on in the pandemic. People loved it.

ime ain't as long as time takes sometimes. Borges would craft a line between Bergsonian and more mystical/religious time, but time ain't got no time for philosophy nor religion. time ignores all ways of life but allows. time is relentless and perseveres but is not impervious. time ain't never been no kind of superhero. Aion is unbounded and mysterious, neutral to the need of prayers while also laying foundations for both joy and misery.

what is love but a reduce, reuse, recycle sort of emotion. will settle for dreams when love is not around. will use dreams, one for one, as a replacement in any recipe.

here's where a quote should be but it ain't coming. the sample called out or called in depending on how one wants to phrase it, if not think about it. either way, no work for the quote on this section. the quote took "advantage" of the policy put in place for these special conditions.

the cento and collage need some time off. the pastiche put in a request for a leave of absence.

can't think straight right now. can't think queer either. can't make a good joke either.

how does one take one's Black? with joy? how does one take one's Afro? with pessimism? it's not a dichotomy. joyful pessimism. pessimistic joy. absurd but not funny.

keeping it real is a spectrum.

it's second summer. it's fall. there once was another name for this. it's a good weekend for a thug holiday. a remembrance and prayer up for those not here no matter how those came to be thought of as thugs.

went to a reading online where the Black speaker said there was no freedom to speak within a mixed company. the written act though not the same as the speech act is likewise incarcerated if not enslaved. each paragraph, the barracoon. the word is of Iberian origin, it's Hispanic Heritage Month. hopefully these will not be the posthumous memoirs of Bras Boricua also glossed as *Epitaph of a Small Loser*.

can't everybody be Keith Moon, but the attempt was made. and now those folks who said that who were legends in the scene as college rock gave way to indie but were punks at heart even in the kitchen even behind the bar are now on patios with reading glasses on noses perusing menus.

one thing read can ruin everything. this is not its original. though to say what changed would further its corruption but a coopting elsewhere removed any similarities here. allies don't understand how narratives are taken and translated from the Aramaic to mouths of evangelicals while always maintaining a sense of, make that a belief in, loyalty.

the news is on at work and this is where the beginning was.

   fatal strategies or revolutionary suicide.

this had more and is now less. it was ruined by its proximity to something else. what was essential to this has been redacted which did not distill this but deformed it. yet, it was necessary so as not to approximate an approval of the ruiner. this is vague. details of certain deaths are not. lists of the infected are not. the attendance policy is not. when a stimulus check will arrive is. tweets are. photos are aleatory even if Wittgenstein said that a picture is a fact. Baudrillard even with camera in hand and notebooks of *Cool Memories* being composed knew that photoshop and filters existed and McLuhan was talking about media not memories but a picture is sort of a rear view. a mirror is not an illusion. the intention of the viewer is. wait, that's not quite wrong but what was meant was *the extension* or maybe *the invention*. where is the disappearance when social death is highly visible and the private survival is imprisoned?

sometimes it is rather similar to that. other times it be more akin to this. it happens to be what happens at the moment. as the sun reaches its nadir, illation accepts a movement towards its apex.

can't suggest further readings. these words as so much those that want also to be understood will assuredly miss the mark. the essay is no place to take a stand.

"To hell with the future. It's a [hu]man-eating idol." —Ivan Illich keeping it real is not the opposite of keeping it illusion. where Lacan is, replace with ... the mirror state was once a mirror settlement. an invasion. where the simulation is, find the simulacra and explain in cinematic terms why being here at work selling everything from TVs to Takis is bullshit. but tampons and something else to keep the alliteration going / the consonance are constant, necessary, and not temporal. yet, and yet, and but more yet to come the role of the stocker, cleaner, and even cashier are not heroic except online. the micro-movies of the mundane made to move by thumbs as scripted by neighbors, strangers, bots, and selves who authenticate identities to log in but de-authenticate under the pressure of the public. the panopticon ... insert Foucault. remove interest.

in grad school, a long meandering poem called into the narrative both Oscar Wilde and Iceberg Slim. in a shorter essay, may both the incarceration of Wilde be not forgotten alongside the breakdown of the con by Slim and the investigation of the death of Melvin X. let also there be room here for the quotes that were removed. let the thug holiday that was at the start of this be here at the end alongside the cabin fever. let the lyrics find a place but not proximity. something something something from Dunbar to Larsen to Outkast to Mulatto. something else something else something else Baqt, Zanj, Dessalines, FALN ... no time. no space. no more argument. no more guessing games. there are no billboards to signal all the little signs. the collapse will not be televised. the memes will be too late. here's a bonus of $300 that all the news outlets know about and will share. meanwhile, depression, anxiety, nor even "actual" symptoms are not any real reason to abuse the attendance policy. Black movies on display at new rollback prices don't mean work can be missed to go protest. and Facebook is being monitored.

On January 13, 2020, my dog Hitchcock ("Hitch") was diagnosed with Multilobular Osteochondrosarcoma. On March 13, 2020, I began working from home because of the coronavirus pandemic. For me, the lockdown, or quarantine, or whatever it is, has meant more time to spend with my dying dog.

Multilobular Osteochondrosarcoma is, in short terms, a bone cancer. Hitchcock's tumor is on the roof of his mouth and, thankfully, it had not spread to his lymph nodes or lungs before it was discovered. Also, thankfully, he was able to get a debulking surgery and his series of radiation treatments completed before the world closed down. So, all that was left was the recuperation.

My work is in the entertainment industry—specifically, the movie business—which has, of course, been severely impacted by COVID-19. By day, I would go to an office and deliver digital files, pushing ones and zeroes around, making sure the content got to all the right places. By night, I would attend movie screenings and write or talk about the films I had seen.

Both of these jobs can be done from home. My laptop is fully capable of moving ones and zeroes around whether I'm at a desk or on a couch. And in-theater movie screenings have been replaced by digital movie screener links, more ones and zeroes delivered to me by studios that I can consume from home. And, from home, Hitchcock can do both of these jobs with me. Or, at least, he can lie down next to me while I do them. And he's a great movie-watching partner.

The blessing of spending time with Hitch hasn't all been lying around and watching movies, though. Another plus to being home with him is that his condition needs near-constant monitoring, something I couldn't give him if I had been going to work. His mass bleeds every once in a while, so I need to keep an eye on him so he doesn't make the house look like a heinous crime scene. He's a sweetheart about it, he approaches either me or my wife when he feels the blood start to drip and lets us know, so the damage is minimal. And the Chinese herbal supplement Yunnan Baiyao works wonders for bleeding, in case anyone was wondering. These bloody incidents rapidly deplete our already-scarce supply of paper towels.

Also, as the tumor grows (as tumors do), there's less room for his tongue in his mouth. So, it just sort of hangs out the side of his jaw, which is totally cute if you don't know the reason behind it. This makes it harder and harder for him to eat. So, I have to feed him the last bites of his meals by hand; and the number of last bites has increased as the mass has grown. He also has trouble drinking, so, there's some mopping up of water to do around his bowl each time after he finishes. Again, not good for our paper towel supply, but a necessary thing to keep him hydrated.

Hitchcock isn't a young dog. He's twelve years old, which is a pretty good run for a boxer. And some of his ailments may be due to his senior age. I've had to set up a ramp for him to get up on the bed with us, which is absolutely where I want him sleeping—right at my feet. At first, he was skeptical; but now, he hits it like a champ. His doctors always ask if he seems lethargic, and I never know what to say. He sleeps all the time, but he's a twelve-year-old boxer, you know? That's what they do. Sleep.

Sometimes in the middle of the night, he'll hop off the bed and move to a couch in another room. If this action wakes me up, I'll move along with him and sleep out there too. Sometimes I wonder if he's going out there to be alone, but he always shares a pillow with me and snuggles up, so I think he appreciates the company. I don't know why he moves out there, but I don't think it's to get away.

This time at home with Hitchcock has been a gift. I have always considered him my emotional support animal, and he has always been there for me when I've been anxious, lonely, or depressed. And I like to think that he welcomes the reciprocation now that he needs it. His companionship also makes being cooped up inside much more tolerable for me. Even when he's sick, he's a giver.

On August 26, 2020, my wife and I were forced to make the decision to send Hitch on his final journey. The pandemic even affected this, as neither his regular vet nor his oncology clinic would allow people inside their hospitals, they would only take him in without us. We owed him more than having his last moments be spent frantically looking around the room for us, so, we had a mobile vet come to our home to perform the procedure.

All things considered, this turned out to be a great decision. First, he was given a sedative to relax. And once that was administered, he climbed up onto the couch with me and we just looked out the window together. When the drugs took effect and he couldn't stay upright anymore, he just slinked down onto his spot on the couch, the same spot where he had been lounging next to me for the last five and a half months, with me right next to him again, holding him, petting him, kissing him. I had my face right next to his when the doctor gave him his final shot of the pink stuff, and he drifted off to sleep. The last thing he saw before going under was my face.

Hitchcock still watches movies with me. Only now, instead of lying on the couch next to me, he's in an ornate wooden box.

I still talk to him, though.

CATASTROPHE MODEL (QUICK NOTES)

RABB ASAD

PERILS MODELED

Earthquake, Extratropical Cyclones (Winter Storms), Flood, Multiple Peril Crop, Pandemic Influenza, Severe Thunderstorm (Tornado, Hail, Straight-line Wind), Terrorism, Tropical Cyclones (Hurricanes, Typhoons, Wildfire)

LATE STAGE CAPITALISM (FOUND)

The debtor has to come up with either a firm commitment for a loan that would cover our payoff or a greater amount from a substantial lender or a purchase and sale agreement from a qualified purchaser acceptable to the lender. One of these two things has to happen by the 31st day of December 2020.

COMPOUND INTEREST, OR DISCRIMINATION

Ten men arriving with two hearts each within ensconce themselves in the 17th floor conference room leather.

THE HAZARD COMPONENT, OR SOOTHSAYER

Where are future events likely to occur? How novel? Catalogs with infinite computer-simulated catastrophes are imagined, representing a range of plausible events.

INSURANCE-LINKED SECURITIES, OR ALL-NIGHTER

Inelegant instruments, we embrace and do the arithmetic of Greenwich, Connecticut.

NASDAQ:TICKER

Numbers flicker: fiat numbers, blood numbers, drug numbers, money is money numbers. Leukemia's cure is good corporate earnings that trickle down to the stock's ticker.

CHILDREN'S MOVEMENT, OR WE HAVE THE POETS!

We want power! We want Kamala Harris on speed dial! We want land and condominiums! We want to occupy the Apple Store! We want stocks, bonds, and blockchain.

CATASTROPHE REFERENCE CHART (HURRICANE)

Saffir-Simpson Hurricane Wind Scale, Category 5, Sustained Winds (MPH) 157 or higher. Catastrophic damage will occur: A high percentage of framed homes will be destroyed, with total roof failure and wall collapse. Fallen trees and power poles will isolate residential areas. Power outages will last weeks to months. Most of the area will be uninhabitable for weeks or months.

THE FINANCIAL COMPONENT

Hurricane Sally, in addition to causing up to $7 billion in insured losses, may leave insurers insolvent.

FAMINE

The ore to feed the blast furnace?

PHOTOSHOPPED

Two boys leave hollows in the earth after they half bury marbles. The boys position the marbles the requisite horizontal distance of fake beauty—a span of two and a half inches by their calculations.

POSTMODERN MOONSCAPE

Snow, treasured up, hails. Empty glass towers eclipse on the skyline like heavenly bodies washed in ice glow.

YES MEN

Compartmentalize the affair on Gmail. Keep collecting zip codes. Deploy the 2nd Battalion, 3rd Infantry Regiment of the 3rd Stryker Brigade, 2nd Infantry Division, at Joint Base Lewis-McChord located south of Seattle.

TORNADO PAINTS LIKE WILLIAM H. JOHNSON

Men place blue tarps across roof rafters. Red rags of cloth and a purple and black bra speckle the acres.

CHIRAQ

And the east border is the east fire.

HOLOGRAM JAMES BALDWIN

Every black man is a gun.

HUMAN CATASTROPHES MODELED

Warfare, Terrorism, Cybersecurity Attacks, Casualty/Liability Events, Displacement Crises

JAZZY IS SO HIGH SHE THINKS SHE HEARD EVERYTHING COLTRANE SAID

I know you are not a drug dealer, but seriously he has a whole bottle of Percocets; and you can sell those for like $20 dollars a pill if you chose.

INDICTMENT, OR ASPIRATION (FOUND)

Upon Conviction of the offense alleged in Count 1 of this Superseding Indictment, the defendants shall forfeit to the United States any and all property, and interest therein, constituting, or derived from, any proceeds obtained directly or indirectly, as a result of the said violation, including but not limited to the follow:

A. SPECIFIC ASSETS

a) The sum of approximately $739,000.00 in United States currency seized from Safe Deposit Box #821 at the Chase Bank branch at 3593

Peachtree Road, Atlanta, Georgia.

b) Articles of jewelry with a total appraised value of $406,950.00 including the following items seized at 2 Avenue of the Americas, New York, New York 10013:

1. One Men's Rolex Oyster Perpetual Day-Date Pearlmaster Chronometer bearing serial #V93527, valued at $60,000.00.
2. One 18-carat yellow gold Christ head with diamonds and set with approximately 325 round brilliant diamonds, valued at $20,000.
3. One Lady's Rolex Oyster Perpetual Pearlmaster bearing serial #Pl199844, valued at $35,000.00.

ESTRANGED

We leave each other like passengers shedding a train's motion at the stop. It's like when you break your lease—the way landlords and tenants just turn their backs on each other. You have to have the stomach for real estate.

FIRST BAPTIST PARKING LOT SERVICE

Tongues, desirous of communion, wag from the windows of SUVs and coupes. Hands and feet dance their confessions.

TABLEAU #1: QUARANTINE TIMELAPSE

The only thing that changes about this tableau is the light. The players are all the same. The set is the same, but the scene starts before day and bellows into dawn and morning and afternoon and evening and into the dark and black night.

LINES OF BUSINESSES MODELED

Commercial Property, Personal Property, Workers' Compensation, Automobile Physical Damages, Limited Liabilities, Product Liabilities, Business Interruptions

SOUTHWEST ATLANTA LOVE LETTER, OR CROP

Before I forget, I finally got the fried corn recipe right, the way they used to make it: Sweet corn, pepper, salt, and butter. You save the milk when you cut the corn from the cob and use that too. Fry everything in a black skillet. I asked Auntie if you can use olive oil and she said yeah. She said use a little sugar too, but I don't know about that. For me, the corn is already sweet. You can add okra and tomato once you finish cooking the corn if you like that.

CATASTROPHE MODEL OUTPUTS

The output is a computer-generated estimate of the losses the model predicts for a single catastrophe or a string of catastrophic events. When generating a probabilistic model, the output is either a probabilistic loss distribution or a set of catastrophic events that could be used to create a loss distribution. When generating a deterministic model, losses caused by a specific event can be calculated with ease. For example, the user could simulate and analyze the effect of a Category 5 Hurricane or a state-sponsored terrorist attack in downtown Mobile, Alabama, against the user's portfolio of exposure.

JOSEPH EDWIN HAEGER

I've been thinking about the moon lately.

Every year, she gets about an inch and a half farther away from us. It's the slowest breakup in the universe and we're meant to sit here and watch it, pretending like she's a constant in our lives, always there from now until forever. Illuminating our nights as a beautiful ornament; shifting our tides so an array of life is washed to and away from us; helping us rotate as we make our long elliptical orbit around the sun.

The moon makes us feel normal.

But, in the end, she's nothing more than a reminder that we're temporary.

At 33, I've seen the moon drift forty-nine inches away—just over four feet. A distance I could make with one big step if I really wanted. From this plane to the next.

When Italo Calvino published "The Distance of the Moon" she was about seven feet closer to us. It makes me wonder if Calvino knew she was bigger in his sky than she would be in mine. Could he imagine how she was going to look, floating up there in the year of our lord 2020? Or was he too preoccupied with thinking about how close she looked hundreds of years before him? Did he even bother to think forward into the future, when the moon will be nothing but a pinprick, rocketing away from her home?

2020 is the year absurdity died. Nothing is funny and nothing matters. Individualism has corroded the American Dream and instead of riding the crest of the wave, we tumbled off long before it even thought about breaking and rolling back. We're being thrown around, hoping to get a calming moment of reprieve, but all we've gotten are wildfires, global viruses, rising sea levels, political unrest, and economic turmoil.

We argue about issues that are nothing more than a slogging step forward or back, not meant to make any meaningful impact in the long term. And one day, the moon will be gone, and our planet will lurch to a halt. We're all going to die, crossing our fingers there's something more than a long black void afterward.

But then I think about the 70,000 kids in cages. About the disproportionate policing of people of color. Roe v Wade. And I realize, these slogging steps might not directly affect me, but goddamn if they don't affect people I love. Then I think—it doesn't even matter if these are people I love or not; these are things that affect human beings.

It's discouraging to find myself slipping into the same individualistic mindset I lob judgements at. It's frightening how easily I can put myself before the collective, but I'm working on it. I'm constantly trying to reprogram myself to recognize the collective over the individual. Because we're all in this together.

Even if the moon drifts away an inch and a half every year, we can all lift up our hands and beckon it to come back. I know it's futile—we're on a one-way ride—but at least we'd be doing it together.

ELLEN YAFFA

I can't live this year as I expected to, and the clock is ticking. What I want is to engage fully with life—to explore, travel, connect, listen, and learn. I'm in the third third of my life and, in the words I heard at the La MaMa Theatre in Greenwich Village last year, now more than ever imprinted on the frontal lobe of my brain, "Time Don't Stop for Nobody."

Don't get me wrong. While I am in a high-risk, stay-at-home COVID cohort—thanks to my personal history spanning seven decades—I get it. I get how fortunate I am; privileged to not be scarred by the random attacker in our midst. The one who snatches essential workers, people of color, and the physically vulnerable, ensnaring them in tentacles they can't even see coming.

But there is a cost to me, too. Even in my healthy, stable base camp, I might lose a year of what provides meaning and purpose in my life. And that is a lot of opportunity wasted.

By mid-March, I had stopped tutoring first-graders struggling to learn how to read and gathering donations for domestic violence survivors. I could fill a suitcase with experiences I was salivating over and almost had this summer. A trip to London for my great nephew's Bar Mitzvah; to Russia for my son's overseas wedding celebration with his new in-laws; hiking the Scottish isles; and finishing the trip in Slovenia. I'm actually now at peace with those losses and, as I look at the list, I feel whiny.

Future lost opportunities are what I fear more than the pile of "did not dos" these past six months. If a reliable vaccine is delayed, will it be more than a year until I see my son and his new wife? Will there be a grandchild in Russia or Berlin whom I cannot meet in person? Will I continue to feel like a version of myself, not the whole person? One who walks around in figurative astronaut boots, feet not always grounded, mind losing focus, aching for the satisfaction of dinner out with friends, museums, movies, live theater. Legs folded under my table at Thanksgiving, family members brushing shoulders and eye rolling.

A nagging anxiety hangs in the air like a fog bank, or carbon monoxide. Stealthy, lurking, a pall unseen. I am a forward-looking person who recharges by stepping into life. Yet, here I am, longing for a retro BC (Before COVID) tempo, with accelerated social and economic justice.

I try to focus on gratitude, and I do have Zen moments. I pursue activities to stimulate my mind and create connection with pursuits and people I love. But what I really want—to resume an in-person life—is elusive. My patience is wearing thin for more months of visiting on Zoom like contestants on *Hollywood Squares*. I'm overdue to use verbs like "go" and "do" and "discover."

I fear the hole being created by lost opportunity; and not having enough time or stamina, when AC (After COVID) comes, to climb out.

for Wendy C. Ortiz

This is from a 2016 interview with the writer Wendy C. Ortiz following the presidential election.

"What comes next, do we all just leave [the country] now?" the interviewer asks.

"You want to be a friend to me? Stay and fight. Otherwise, you're of no use," Ortiz responds.

It is an exchange I return to time and time again. It is also how I choose to think about 2020.

To look at 2020 in all its parts and enormity feels impossible.

Work. COVID. Inequity. Parenting. Racism. Domestic terrorism. Lies. Anger. Violence. Hate. Remote learning. Inequality. Fear. Illness. Protest. Rioting. QAnon. Police brutality. Voter suppression. Fire. Death.

I am reminded of Anne Lamott's book *Bird by Bird*. Lamott is a child. Her brother has to do a report for school cataloging the birds in their backyard. He's waited until the last moment. There are too many birds and too much work. He's overwhelmed.

Lamott's mother says, "Relax, we'll write the report bird by bird."

Small things. The big picture can be too big, too much.

And so it is that, instead of looking at 2020 in all its parts and enormity, I choose to start by looking at 2016 and the interview I listened to with author (and friend) Wendy C. Ortiz. Ortiz is being interviewed in the wake of the presidential election and the interviewer says, "What are we supposed to do now, just leave?" The question is plaintive, fraught with concern, and real, or real enough for many.

Let me digress for a moment.

The other day, I saw an anguished tweet by a one-time conservative commentator, now Never Trumper, in which he asked, "Is this what all of you expected?"

The *you* as being those of us who were filled with dread and sadness following the results of the 2016 presidential election. Those of *us* who believed that a vote for Trump was a vote for hate. Point blank. Full stop. Period.

I posted as much to my Facebook page the morning after the results were in.

Some high school friend's friend responded, "I don't hate anyone."

I replied with what I still believe to be true, "Your vote tells a different story."

However, what I better appreciate now is that hate may be hate but failing to examine the origins of the anger (that some portion of the body politic feels towards those in charge and Hillary Clinton as a representative of that) and why that anger exists serves no one. It's part of the reason we've arrived here.

People feel left behind, replaced, ignored. They feel the country they love is slipping away. And while *that* country is one many of us are thrilled to see slip away (one rife with racism, homophobia, classism, anti-Semitism, xenophobia, and misogyny), we need to recognize that our leaders don't seem to care much about those left behind until their anger boils over.

Trump well understands that anger and he's been happy to massage, stoke, and exploit it.

Returning to that tweet ... "Is this what all of you expected?"

Yes. And fuck yes.

Though, it's worse than I imagined.

Still, is it easier or preferable to leave?

"You want to be a friend to me? Stay and fight. Otherwise, you're of no use," Ortiz replied.

So, that has been my first step to approaching 2020. *Stay and fight.* Which is what 2020 has been for most of us: one long fight. To be healthy. To stay employed. To parent. To teach. To find glimmers of hope. And joy.

But also, to fight back. To not be discouraged. To remember that it didn't have to be this bad. What 2020 has become is not an aberration. It's not some weird, terrible, contortion of random events that leaves us here, now, perplexed and fucked.

At this moment some might say, "What? No, that's exactly what COVID is, a weird, terrible, contortion of random events that leaves us here, now, perplexed and fucked."

Yes, COVID itself was not expected, and, yes, every disease and pandemic has its own unique traits, characteristics, and path. However, governments can learn from the past, project what is to come, embrace a sense of urgency (and science) when those horrors arrive, and craft a nationwide plan in response. This administration has failed the country on all of these counts.

And yet, while I don't know how the pandemic will end, or why people can't wear fucking masks, what has most often caused me pause during this time is how entrenched inequity and racism (and classism) are in the institutions purported to protect the people of this country.

Decent healthcare is inaccessible to those who are most vulnerable, and primarily coupled with employment. Men and women of color are disproportionately brutalized, arrested, and shot. Many essential jobs are low-paying and dangerous. Decent, safe, and stable housing is scarce. Our immigration policies are broken, capricious, and cruel. The right to vote is under constant attack and suppressed.

I knew all of this *before* 2020 and have reflexively fought against these things throughout my adult life. They're not right. The data is clear. These institutions must be fixed. Blown up, if needed. But did I think about how any of it worked (and did not)? Or what any of it meant to those most impacted by it?

Not enough. Which is privilege. The privilege of not being personally affected by much of it and not having to think deeply about most of it.

Did I know I was privileged before 2020? *Yes.* Did I consciously make changes to my lifestyle and think about addressing this? *I'm not sure.*

I am reminded of an interview with one of Tom Brady's former teammates after Brady was quoted as saying that what he loved about football locker rooms is that they're colorblind.

The teammate said, that's the problem, we don't want Tom Brady to be colorblind, we want him to understand our differences, ask questions, listen, and, if needed, give up some of what he has.

Being colorblind is a privilege. Not having to seek out answers and understanding is privilege. Being unwilling to give up any of what you have is privilege. Being able to leave and not fight, even feeling like that's an option, is privilege.

All of which is how I think about 2020 and what comes next.

I have a lot to learn. I have a lot to do. I have an obligation to stay and fight.

ARE MY CARNAL RHYMES THE CURE FOR MY PORN ADDICTION?

ADRIAN ERNESTO CEPEDA

That is the million-dollar question. If I had the answer, I wouldn't necessarily be wealthy, but I would feel richer through enlightenment.

Let me stop lollygagging and skirting the issue. My porn addiction became a serious concern, thanks to the free premium account Pornhub offered during quarantine. Sadly, my cravings began around the time mi mami died. [Paraphrasing Ron Jeremy when referencing masturbation: I don't blame porn or Pornhub. Any way you self-satisfy is a natural thing and like a famous New York director once said, "Don't knock masturbation. It's sex with someone you really love."] This essay is not against porn nor masturbation; it's about how I tried to use my addiction as a release for the pain and grief I was trying not to feel.

The quick and easy answer, which soon became a determinant in my life, was to self-soothe by watching a video of one of my favorite porn stars on YesPornPlease—a website that no longer exists, by the way, in case anyone tries to look this website up. Because I was not dealing with the death of my parent, the one genre of porn that I would achieve the maximum self-pleasure was watching erotic scenes with older women, or MILFs. I realize now that there should have been warning bells and signs going off, but at that time I just needed a jolt of pleasure to ease the pain of a loss that I did not want to feel or face on the inside.

You must remember, this is still a time before COVID, I was still self-satisfying only in my office at home. Like Lou Reed once said, "How do I stay creative? I masturbate every day. OK!" It was part of my daily routine, to open my mind and stimulate myself creatively watching porn before breakfast and driving on the 110 commuting to work and having a normal life in denial of any of the issues that were hidden away not trying to face the death of mi mami. I was also busy promoting the one of three poetry collections, and a poetry chapbook, along with focusing on planning, editing, and hosting a panel on LatinX poets at the AWP (Association of Writers and Writing Programs) Conference in San Antonio. Besides writing, working, promoting my book(s), I spent a year on that panel, it was the one thing that I put all my energies toward. Thankfully, it was a success. But once the panel was done, all my focus, which went towards promoting my new poetry book, there was a gap that needed filling.

Enter the pandemic, and now I had more time to not face the reality of mi mami's death. This meant more time for my porn addiction. Because of this and many porn websites offering free premium memberships (I do not blame any adult-film service, this was my own addiction), I needed more and more release to cover up the pain, the emptiness that I was avoiding on the inside. Sadly, the more I watched, the less pleasure I experienced. There was no self-soothing. There was nothing but shame as I quickly lost grip of my addiction; I was trying to fulfill an impenetrable gap and I was experiencing anything but satisfaction.

I remember a moment after I experienced my physical, emotional, and mental breakdown, where one day I decided to go back and dive into that addiction. It was a mistake because as soon as I gripped that desire inside that rabbit hole, the depression hit me worse. It was no longer fun. It made me feel worthless, like I had no self-control. I used to lie to myself and claim that I was a connoisseur of the adult-film arts. *Nice try*. I had an addiction which I used to mask the pain of not facing the traumatic death of mi mami. It was no longer about any kind of satisfaction, it was all about trying to feed the habit that had taken over my life, and there was no joy, no arousal, just pain that I needed to come to grips with.

Cut to more recently. I had a feeling, a desire to go back and watch a porn clip, and I think I found an answer for this craving … instead of breaking down, I ordered a photography book by Francesca Woodman called *Being an Angel*. I realized, instead of giving in to this addiction, why not look at Francesca's photographs, which do include subjects naked? [Some might consider the images risqué, I call it art.] So, my answer was to craft ekphrastic poems. My specialty, a form of poetry that is inspired by a photograph or artwork. So, I wrote a poem from one of Francesca's photographs and it worked, I wrote about my admiration for her work. I had a new creative outlook, I started to see her photos not simply as titillating but also as stunning works of art.

Channeling my carnal energies by writing poetry worked, but what will happen when I start taking my anti-anxiety medication? Will my sex drive lessen? Will this also diminish my porn addiction? Whatever happens, I am hoping my passion for writing ekphrastic poetry will only increase with my desire.

Writing these poems was only the first step to my treatment. Luckily, because of my mental health issues, I am recovering, talking to a therapist, and taking anti-anxiety medications. At first, I was worried because I feared taking any medication would stifle any creative outlet and lessen my sex drive, but the opposite happened. Thankfully, because of my daily treatment regimen, I am calmer, and my internet addiction faded away.

The first thing I do every morning is write a letter to connect with my dead mami and this helps. Best of all, I don't need the hub of Porn anymore. I watched a clip the other day and all those obsessive emotions have faded. The good news is that the treatment is working. I don't need to watch porn clips to become aroused to try to cover up the pain of her death anymore. Best of all, one of the positive side effects of my medication, and much to my wife's delight, is that I wake up aroused and ready to go. Needless to say, we connect intimately in the shadows before the sun rises and it is very caliente.

I want to reiterate that there is nothing wrong with watching porn or masturbating. My addiction was linked to not facing my issues of death and using porn to try to mask and cover up these feelings by self-soothing to try to find release. Sadly, all I found was emptiness and more pain.

Thankfully, porn is no longer a trigger. It started with me coming to grips for the reasons of my addiction. It has been a wild journey that started with a click, a clip, and ended with therapy and medication. Best of all, I am connecting more with my wife, mi mami through the letters that I write her daily, and I am channeling the rest of my eroticism by crafting ekphrastic poems from photographers like Francesca Woodman and Sanne Sannes. Instead of seeing sexual objects, I look at these photos with the eye of an ignited artist that is ready to reflect erotic poetry on every line (and even more amorous climaxes, on and off the page).

JASON ZENOBIA

September 30th, 2020

Dear Person or Persons of the theoretical future:

A s this year's motto, I offer for your consideration: "Oh, crap! What NOW!?"

Part of the reason I have waited as long as possible to submit my thoughts (today was the deadline) is because this year is so vast and varied in its horrors that whatever I write will be antiquated within seconds.

If you are reading this in the future (assuming there is one), you will have the benefit of hindsight and have already lived through the rest of this ~~dreadful~~ ~~ghastly horrible~~ challenging year. I can hear you saying, "The end of September? He hadn't even seen the swarms of flaming, locust-wasp-spiders that ate people's eyeballs right out of their sockets! What the hell does he know?" (Thanks, Monsanto!)

Also, it's really hard for me to get my shit together, especially since washing my hands and not panicking have become full-time occupations. Although, it turns out I've been sheltering in place my whole life. I just didn't know it was called that, or that it had such utility. Germaphobes have been ahead of this curve the whole time, and so have I.

One plus side of this Global Pandemic is that wearing a facemask in public prevents others from seeing my lips move when I talk to myself. I am, therefore, less likely to be identified as insane by passers-by. But, to make up for it, my barber shop is closed. My hair and beard have reached a state envied by twisted loners crafting their manifestos in shacks the world over.

As it stands today, the whole world smells like a gin and tonic due to the abundance of hand sanitizer. This pairs nicely with a phrase I've heard a lot recently: "Good God! I need a drink!" But please do not drink your hand sanitizer, nor bleach. Even if the psychotic dumbshit in the Oval Office thinks it would be "The Greatest."

And speaking of the malevolent nonsense poem who occupies the Oval Office:

Actually, let's not go there.

Let's see … Is there anything funny about the end of the world?

I'll let you know as soon as I'm done crafting my manifesto.

… and washing my hands.

Again.

OCTOBER 2020

OCTOBER 2 – Trump and First Lady test positive for COVID-19; Trump enters hospital.

OCTOBER 8 – White House COVID-19 outbreak grows to 34.

OCTOBER 8 – West Health-Gallup poll reveals that more Americans trust Biden to lead US health care system through pandemic.

OCTOBER 8 – The FBI charges 13 militiamen with plotting to kidnap Michigan Governor Gretchen Whitmer at her vacation home. [A 14th suspect is arrested on October 15.]

OCTOBER 10 – Trump on coronavirus: "But it's going to disappear; it is disappearing."

OCTOBER 12 – Trump on coronavirus: "I went through it. Now, they say I'm immune. I can feel—I feel so powerful."

OCTOBER 22 – Trump on coronavirus: "We are rounding the turn. We are rounding the corner."

OCTOBER 23 – Arkansas and Oregon set single-day records for new coronavirus cases.

OCTOBER 24 – Michigan, Illinois, New Mexico, and Ohio all set single-day records for new coronavirus cases.

OCTOBER 26 – Walter Wallace Jr. is shot and killed by two police officers in Pennsylvania.

OCTOBER 27 – Pennsylvania, Wisconsin, and Kentucky reach new single-day records for new coronavirus cases.

OCTOBER 29 – Michigan, Oregon, and Illinois report new single-day records for new coronavirus cases.

OCTOBER 30 – The FBI launches an investigation into an incident in Texas where a Joe Biden campaign bus tour was canceled after a caravan of supporters of President Trump attempted to run it off the road and hit a staffer's car.

237,192 DEATHS | 9,495,787 INFECTED

'be always been poor, but I've always been a hustler. Hustling, in the long run, allows you to overcome everything. In 2019, my hustle was starting to pay off. For the first time in my life, I had three jobs and knew where the money to pay my bills was going to come from. After losing sleep under the oppressive shadow of eviction twice in my life, knowing money was coming in steadily felt great. But that was only half of it.

Things were also going well in my writing career, the thing I've been trying to achieve for the past decade. I sold two novels in France and the publisher was going to fly me there for a tour of five cities in early 2020. I was writing for some of my favorite venues and getting paid for it. I was traveling around the country doing readings and getting paid to give keynote speeches about diversity in publishing. I gave talks and readings in Houston, Oxford, Marquette, Austin, Chicago, Baltimore, San Antonio, Denver, and other cities. I went to New York to be part of a writers' room for a cool project. Things were moving. In fact, I was traveling so much I had to take personal days off at work because I used all my PTO early in the year.

In November 2019, I stood on an NYC sidewalk at 2:00 a.m. and thought, *Wow, this is awesome. I'm going to do everything in my power to make 2020 better.*

Enter 2020 ... and COVID-19.

The world came to a grinding halt, and my career went with it. Every bit of momentum I'd gained suddenly vanished. The conferences I'd been invited to? Canceled. The workshops I was supposed to give in Canada? Canceled. The readings all across the country? Canceled. The French tour? Canceled. Instead of traveling, I was stuck at home, silently watching the death of my career's momentum and feeling powerless.

I focused on myself and then was forced to look around because people were dying. That was worse than anything that had happened to me. That was awful. No career matters more than a human life. My heart broke all over again. Then, it got worse.

The pandemic changed people. Folks whose intelligence I respected became COVID deniers. People I'd hung out with started talking about how wearing a mask was an attack on their freedom. And that was only the start of the stupidity. As the weeks rolled by, I watched the country split into groups that had nothing to do with socioeconomic status. The Disunited States of America became a thing. The number of cases kept growing. Comparisons between the United States and other countries exposed how useless the current administration was. The economy collapsed. Momentum died for everything and everyone. Little did we know the year was only getting started.

June rolled around and I lost my main job. The bit of financial stability I'd come to rely on was gone. The hit brought back everything that had happened to me since the beginning of the year. The death of my momentum and the death of the country's momentum were similar, and the maggots that feasted on the carcasses were the same.

Hustling teaches you many things. How to cope is one of them. What do you do when the bodies pile up? How do you process unrelenting negativity? Where do you put a crippling sense of helplessness? What do you do when you can't do anything? The answer was clear: hustle.

With three jobs, finding time to write was almost impossible. In 2019, I had managed to write about 45,000 words of a novel. I wrote at airports and motels. I wrote at my kitchen table in the middle of the night. I wrote while taking breaks from grading. Now, I had more time. There was less work, less traveling, and no money. If you want something, the only thing you can control is the amount of work you put in to get it, and remembering that helped me cope with the ugliness enveloping the country. I was hurting, so I hustled.

Fiction allows us to tell the truth through lies. Fiction is a mirror we hold up to the world. Fiction is entertainment in times of despair. Fiction is one of the tools we have to obliterate ignorance, attack racism, and discuss pain, inequality, and real-life horrors.

With rampant racism mixing in with desperation, the downfall of our economy, and the temporary closure of the world as we knew it, I turned to writing to help me cope. In two months, I wrote about 45,000 words, the same amount it'd taken me more than a year to get on paper the previous year, edited the novel, and found an agent for it. I wrote for new venues. I read even more than usual. COVID had killed our collective momentum and I saw it as other writers struggled with releases during the worst of the pandemic. However, I knew one thing for sure: storytelling is how we survive as a species, so storytelling is the perfect tool to deal with the pandemic.

Our ancestors told stories around the fire as hungry beasts circled them, shining pupils full of menace swimming in a sea of shadows. They fearlessly told and later wrote stories while war raged on, pandemics decimated them, political upheaval changed their world, oppressors made them miserable and tried to silence them, and boats took them to new lives elsewhere, away from everything they knew and loved.

We are storytelling animals, and that is more powerful than the division we're seeing, the stupidity that angers us, and the individuals that govern us. We are storytelling animals, and that means that we keep writing no matter what. Writing is how we survive, how we move forward, how we remember, how we map out a better future. Take the bones of your momentum and write a new story about them. Don't stop. Go write.

OVERVIEW

In January of 2020[1], many Americans voiced an unexpected optimism about the year which quickly imploded into a deep blackhole of fire, plague, masks, quarantine, death, and social unrest exasperated by a chauvinist, authoritarian White Supremacist President. At present, too many people and standards have died and there are no bars to commune with those still mourning. The news is a glass rectangle. The President has the virus and gun stores are out of stock.

Interviews in the following study will focus on the experience of new and intermediate participants in what is now a shit show.

"The Study" was approved as an experimental essay by University of Hell in 2020 and will not adhere to ethical principles of the Declaration of Helsinki and Human Biomedical Research Ethical Issues and Policy Guidance.

The reader will act as the principal investigator and will supervise the management of all data interpretation, statistical analysis, and results dissemination.

ASSUMPTIONS

You will have additional questions that may never be answered. Results will not be collected. Conclusions may vary.

STUDY GOALS

This study seeks to acknowledge that this has been the worst year in many readers' lives and that life is a process full of breath, hope, failures, growth, restarts, success, crying, and, sometimes, sourdough. To that end, questions will focus on topics that allow us to:

Evaluate the impact of "the before" on the expectations of the new now.

Discover: What is the new now? What does it look like? What barriers persist in a social environment rife with the obsession of power amidst the needs of a massive group of people shouldering the conveniences of the fortunate? How do you sleep at night? How does anyone? What can we do to alleviate these aches, these fears?

Assess: Can America survive 2020? Are there moments regarded as useful? Do we know what to do next?

METRICS FOR SUCCESS

2020's goal is for more than 7 out of every 10 participants to achieve the following[2]: sleeping at night[3], working, having something to look forward to, protesting without being gassed, touching literally anyone else, breathing clean air, and believing that the youngest people you know will have the opportunity to be as or more happy than you have been in life.

Or, hope. Just. Hope.

FORMAT

Study participants will consist of an unknowable, but likely small, number of individuals who happen upon this content and have maintained a level of interest that breaches the attention boundaries of modern social media.

Evaluation will be conducted remotely with an interactive prototype over a shared language with the following recruitment guidelines:

- All participants must have a memory of the "before"
- At least half of participants must want to question everything

This interview will be self-moderated and self-answered. All interviews will follow the same general flow, as per the script provided. They'll be conducted in a conversational manner and will gravitate toward necessary themes that catch the attention of the reader. Questions about *how your parents loved you* or other universal *par-for-the-course of life pains* have been omitted in this study.

No records of the interview will be required or collected. Should a participant have issues with understanding *The Study*, they will be free to leave at any time.

IMPLICATIONS FOR RESEARCH
COLLECTION METHODS

Warning: You should know, this will not be an easy road. No one will hear your thoughts when the door opens—notice what you notice. Memories will be broken and fragmented and blurry. No one will save you from what you find there/here—best to grab a drink or a blanket. *Be prepared: you may also find light in a world of pain.*

SCRIPT

The following script will be used to help the researcher guide the participant through exploration of experiences and perceptions of 2020. Notes for the researcher are in brackets.

[INTRODUCTION - 2M]

The session will take as long as you want or need. We don't have a break scheduled, so you'll need to take care of that on your own.

It's important that you express your honest opinion about everything today. We want to know what works well for 2020, but also what's fucked, so please just give your honest opinion ... this is about your experience, so there are no wrong answers.

Finally, I'd like to remind you that you are here on an entirely voluntary basis and may leave or refuse to respond to any question at any time in the interview.

Do you have any questions before we start? [Wait for confirmation.]

[BACKGROUND - 10M]

Tell me the story of "the before". Tell me everything. Can you remember? What was it like to stand in a sea of conversation, to drive to work? Where did you go to laugh? What did you look forward to? Tell me about your hair and what your mom smelled like.

[Have patience.]

How would your friends have described you, then? [Can you remember your friends?] *Give me three faces you loved last year.*

What did you do when you got lonely? Can you give me an example? What did you do when you got bored? Tell me about tunnel vision. [Tell me about frustration and the tragedy of impedance; tell me about crimes of inaction and dead-end jobs and lists. Tell me about the dreams you wished you had. Were you trying to escape back then? Did you know the stars by name?]

What have you forgotten? Who/what do you worry you'll forget?

[INITIAL EXPERIENCE WITH "THE BEFORE" - 7M]

Where were you when you noticed things had <u>definitely</u> changed? Tell me about the empty shelves at the grocery store and the empty bars and the empty preschool playground, about the ghostly streets and curfews.

Who did you talk to first? [Do you remember the words you used?] *What did you buy and lend? Who did you say goodbye to?*

How long did you think this would last? [A month or two?] *Did you or a friend make masks for the medics? Do you still believe what you knew then?* [Should you?]

What did you start and stop eating? How did you get what you ate? Tell me about drinking. [Describe the loud tin chatter of your recycling bin.] *Tell me about the couch.*

[Did your body quake sometimes at night? Did your hands ever shake in the morning?] *Tell me about far-off places and the take-me-with-you.*

Tell me about the silence and the crippling loneliness. Tell me about marriage or dating. Tell me about trust. [To want to fight or scrub the floors is natural. You are here to observe.]

Tell me about lines: busy phone lines for unemployment and lines to buy toilet paper, party lines, and the new ones aging your face. How long did you have to wait to hear a "no"?

Tell me about the long pause, the fingers crossed for a late big check. And, if the payment came, what did you do? Did you get a new laptop or pay back late rent?

Tell me about YouTube.

[EMOTIONAL REACTION TO INSTABILITY - 6M]

When was the first time you had to tell yourself or someone else "no" because of the events of 2020? When was the last time you had to tell yourself or someone else "no" because of the events of 2020? How many times will you have to tell yourself or someone else "no" because of the events of 2020?

[Give it space.]

Please use this space to describe how these events have impacted you.

How are you feeling? Do you have any of the following: fever or chills, cough, shortness of breath or difficulty accepting authority, body aches, new loss of hope or sanity, sore throat or rage?

Have you injected bleach in the last six months? How many times have you washed your hands? Tell me what "clean" means.

Tell me about control.

Tell me about power. Who has it? Why? Tell me about the truth and debates with neighbors. Did you do shots for Ruth Bader Ginsburg?

And, when the recordings came out, did you protest? Did you riot? Did you call a friend or quietly make a sign for your window? Tell me about gas mask sales on Amazon and naked ladies in the street. Tell me about fists thrust at the sky and Proud Boys standing by for the President. Tell me about guns. Tell me about anxiety.

And when the fires ate the air, how bad did it get before you or a loved one left? Tell me about the headaches and the box fan filters. Tell me about the smoke in kitchens and lungs, about the friend's sister who lost everything. How do/can you feel about their loss?

[Notice the way shoulders rise, a tightened jaw, a rub of the arm or palm. Lean forward.]

Tell me about missing your city while never moving homes, or, about a loved one dying a hundred miles away. Alone. Tell me about losing everything. [How many of your communities have died? Tell me about shutting down. Tell me everything.] *Tell me more.*

[Notice the way the shoulders cave and the eyes grow distant. Wait for the second long silence. This is a process.]

Tell me what you're afraid you'll lose next.

Have you touched anyone yet?

[THE "NEW NOW" - 6M]

Do you know what day it is?

    How do you sleep at night? How's your back? How's your family? Tell me.

    How long do you think you can handle this? How long do you think it will last? [Reflect.] *Will you go to the gym or the doctor? Will you get your old life back?*

    How about your job? Do you get to work from home? Tell me about Zoom and sweatpants. Tell me about guilt. Or, tell me about standing behind Plexiglas and a mask in fear of plague and violence. Tell me about the bus. Tell me about meatpacking and food delivery and the ER and the classroom.

    Tell me about parenting in a pandemic. How many teachers do you know? What have you learned about homeschooling? Or, does your kid roam contagious halls? Tell me about safety. Tell me about choice. Tell me about your vote.

    Tell me about America. Do you have a back-up plan? Go on, explain. Or, do you plan to stay? Tell me your thoughts on cops. Tell me about reform.

    How are you dealing with stress? Have you medicated, meditated, and/ or practiced gratitude? Have you made new friends begrudgingly? Have you met your neighbors?

    What are good things about now? Show me the talents you dusted off and what new hobbies you started (and failed)? How's your sourdough? How's your song? Have you gone camping or discovered a park?

    Tell me about yourself, again. Tell me how you've been strong. How much have you grown? [Show me your battle scars.]

    Now, what do you think "okay" means? How do we get to "okay"?[4] How important are these things to you? In what small ways can we start? [Take notes. Make lists.] *Who will you ask for help? How will you maintain hope?*

[RANKING/RATINGS - 3M]

Please listen to the following statements. For each, I'd like you to tell me how you feel about them on a scale of 1-5, where 1 means "I very much disagree" and 5 means "I very much agree":

The hard things I've learned about myself and the world in 2020 will be useful to me in the future.

If I can't make 2020 better for myself, I can do it for someone else.

I will wear a goddamn mask.

I will vote. I will protest. I will use my voice.

I will practice being grateful.

I will call someone I love.

I will try to not give up.

I will not hoard toilet paper.

I will try to exercise and get more sleep.

I will ask for help.

I will offer help.

Things will get better.

We will get through this.

[QUESTIONS/COMMENTS & GOODBYE - 3M]

Do you wish to share any additional comments on the topic of this study? Go on. Tell me more.

Do you have any questions? [I wish I could hear you. I wish I knew.]

Thank you. [Thank you.[5]]

DATA DISSEMINATION

"The Study" was reviewed and approved by L. Davidson, a few inspiring people, and at least one sober editor. Written informed consent was not signed or obtained from participants or their relatives. Results of *The Study* will be interpreted and disseminated by the reader on an anecdotal basis, maybe over beers with friends.

FOOTNOTES

1.   The beginning of the year is colloquially referred to as "the before", as if we have collectively and unconsciously embraced the apocalyptic B-movie nature of our predicament.

2. The following are not included: farmer's markets or promotions of any kind. The bar, here, is low.
3. This includes but is not limited to sleeping without the cops breaking down your door and shooting you.
4. Author openly acknowledges that saying "a less shitty year" feels more appropriate, but now is not the time.
5. There's a bunch of us out here feeling the same way, doing the same things. Even if we're hard to find, keep looking. We've got you.

JACKIE SHANNON HOLLIS

I wake and reach for my husband. Sometimes he's there, asleep, his breath slow and quiet. I let my own breath go slow and quiet. This is what we want. This is what we've been working toward. Him asleep through the night.

Sometimes the blankets on Bill's side are thrown back. He'll be out in the front room, having had another bout of wakefulness. Reading, or maybe he'll have gotten sleepy enough from reading that he's stretched out on the couch and finally, *finally*, fallen to sleep. Eventually he'll find his way back to bed.

Either way, this is progress. This is better than it's been in ten months.

But worry bullies my dreams. In one dream, Bill and I are in Mexico City and we lose each other and I run up and down the streets searching for him. In another, a man with a yard full of smiling golden retrievers holds one of them between his legs and cuts open her chest, pulling back her coat to reveal a bloody monster, wild-eyed, long-fanged.

This is when I reach again for Bill. This is when I go out to the front room and find him asleep on the couch. Sleeping so deeply that he doesn't hear me.

Our house smells of smoke from the wildfires that blew up all over the west coast and came to Oregon with winds that desiccated the leaves, dried the air to dust, turned the sky a dangerous ash-filled orange that has kept everyone indoors.

I turn and go back to the bedroom, past the small safe with our important papers, bags filled with medications, vitamins, and other necessities we packed just in case we have to go fast. Portland is known for her trees. Our house is backed by a forest. Pretty, but way too dry now in early September. A half-million Oregonians are on evacuation notice. Not us. Not yet. But the smoke presses in.

A year ago, in the summer, I was in the lead-up to the launch of my memoir. And in the fall and winter, I was promoting my book. Events every week, all my attention on schedules and interviews and this exciting moment.

Somewhere in the earlier months, Bill went out for lunch with his brother and his brother choked on a piece of chicken. Bill, a retired firefighter and paramedic, had to perform the Heimlich. After a few tries it worked, but all the other times of saving and not saving people from fires and accidents rose up. Old trauma. He began to wake in the night. He began to worry, *what if he hadn't saved his brother?* He got a cold. Then, he got a lung infection. Then, headaches kept him awake. One night in a row, then two. Three.

Things got worse while I was looking the other way. In our thirty-three years, he'd had times of not sleeping perfectly. Episodes of headaches. Nothing new here. By the time I realized how bad things were for him, they were very bad. Most nights, he slept only one or two hours. Some nights, no sleep at all. He stopped being interested in food, in people, in anything outside of himself.

Insomnia became the king of our house; it took over every conversation as we searched for solutions. Bill was desperately tired in the daytime, but Googling said to avoid naps. At night, he became alert and anxious. Deep-breathing and meditation made him more so. He tried more melatonin and less melatonin and stayed awake all night. CBD tincture made him sick. The sauna before bed overheated him and he panicked. One drug helped him fall asleep but not stay asleep, and his hands began to shake and his eyes became so dry that removing his contact lenses required a tiny suction cup.

When I held that tiny suction cup with one hand and his eyelid open with the other, I tried to joke about how drama works like this. Life is normal, then a problem comes along. Each solution creates a new problem. But when my hand trembled too and the tiny suction cup landed on his eye and not the lens, neither of us laughed.

The next drug made him even more wakeful but with a dollop of insanity. That night, his eyes looked like the black and white spirals of some crazy cartoon cat, and I was afraid I'd lost him. That this was the way he would be forever.

Someone had to stay calm. That night, I took him outside. It was Christmas Eve. From midnight to two, we walked back and forth on the sidewalk, me with a flashlight in one hand, him holding my other hand.

"I don't know what's happening to me," he said.

The foggy thinking, the easy anger, the panic of not sleeping, the hopelessness. I didn't know what was happening to him either. I spoke to him about the shapes of trees, the sliver of moon, the sparkly lights on the eaves of that house. The night sounds. Trying to distract him until he felt calm enough to come back inside.

That night, he eventually slept. But three more nights of no sleep fueled his desperation, and I couldn't calm him this time. An emergency room visit led to daily counseling sessions and more medication. Each day, he came home from those sessions with lists of things to do and this overwhelmed him, but he followed each step, trying to get better.

Through the nights, I went in and out of sleep. Sometimes, I sat with him. Sometimes, I went back to bed. I was exhausted too. Sometimes, I was impatient. *Why wouldn't he just sleep?*

Finally, his naturopathic doctor found a medication that gave us hope. He had one good night, then two. Then, another bad night.

She said, "It took you a while to get to this point, it will take time to get better."

He kept on with a delicate balance of medications and sleep hygiene. Rational thinking about this thing called "insomnia."

By late February, the solutions were beginning to work. Four hours, five, some nights even seven. I began to let down my worries. He wanted to eat again and find the weight he'd lost, down to 148 pounds on his six-foot frame. I ordered bags of granola. I felt hope. We were headed out of the dark forest that drama walks through.

Then, a problem came that had nothing to do with the solution. A terror from the outside. Global. A pandemic. We closed in on ourselves, stopped going out, stopped seeing friends and family. I was afraid again. I would be alone with Bill's insomnia.

But we were not alone in being alone. Next door, our neighbor grieved from the death of her husband a month earlier and we couldn't gather for a celebration of his life. A friend with cancer had to sit alone for his chemo treatment while his partner waited in the car. Another friend lost her best friend, clear across the country, from the virus, and could not go be with her. My brother, single and childless, counted on going out for social contact, and suddenly he was alone. My sister couldn't see her grandkids. Nieces juggled work from home, kids at home. The circle of these stories grew outward from our center. We were all in this. People we knew and people we didn't know, the invisible risks. The long unknowns.

I found comfort in seeing my friends in square boxes on the screen, long emails, letters and art in the mail, masked visits on the porch. I began learning the ukulele and, for the first time in many months, Bill would be smiling in the mornings when he came into the room where I was playing.

He said, "I love that sound."

Maybe this was our plot twist. The problem creating a solution. Night after night, without the complication of saying "no" to the people and events we used to say "yes" to. Bill could do all those sleep hygiene things: a consistent pattern, a bath, a quiet read, find a soothing breath practice that actually worked. He ate the granola every morning, taking in the calories, slowly finding the weight he'd lost, and regrouping from the deterioration of thinking that comes with severe insomnia.

Bill began turning his attention outside of himself and onto this new world of 2020, one I'd been keeping at bay while he struggled his own battles. Together, we could speak of the virus, the deaths, the protests, the coming election, the fires.

I've never much liked the idea of silver linings as a balance for hard times. Still, I look for connections. Something that makes it okay to feel the relief that things are better for Bill and me, despite what is happening in the world around us.

We are not at the end of the rippling impact that the world will know for years. And there is our own long trail of a story, Bill's and mine. The smoke in the air is a harbinger of things to come. We should expect sequels, personal and global.

But for now, on this night of smoke and fires, my husband, who once fought such fires, is asleep.

T here are so many layers being peeled back by the events and circumstances of 2020, revealing not only what lies beneath the surface and at the core of many of our fellow countrymen, but also forcing us to look at what lies within ourselves.

Though introspection is old hat for me, the year of COVID has my inner monologue digging a little deeper, asking questions that seem to carry much more weight in these uncertain times. The most significant of these questions for me, the question that speaks to not only how I am perceived by others but also who I perceive myself to be: Where do I fit in? More specifically: How does a refugee baby, grown into a self-aware, middle-aged member of the citizenry, define themselves in terms of the current global socio-political dynamic?

Charlie? Or Chuck?

Commie? Or Gook?

Refugee? Or Traitor?

What kind of Asian are you, anyhow?

Jap? Chink? Other?

A square peg in a slant eye.

I have struggled with my "otherness" for as long as I can remember being self-aware. This otherness was not only a product of genetics, but also of circumstance. I was fortunate in the most unfortunate of circumstances.

Born to young parents in a war-torn country, in a city whose impending collapse would mark the end of said war. I was eight months old when my dad's family got word that the US military was preparing to abandon Sai Gon, and that we should head to the airport immediately, leaving everything behind, to be evacuated as refugees. My father's cousin had married a US Marine, my Uncle Bob, who was the one who arranged for our family to board a C-2 cargo plane bound for Guam. Our group included most of my dad's immediate family—his mom, his six siblings (ranging from late-teens to mid-twenties), and a few cousins, one of whom was pregnant. [On a side note, my paternal grandfather, who worked for the South Vietnamese government, died about ten years earlier in a restaurant bombing, while meeting with US military. This incident would later be depicted in the film *Good Morning, Vietnam*.] We would eventually end up at Camp Pendleton, among the first group of refugees to be placed there. There are pictures somewhere from my first birthday party, which was held in one of the barracks. I was, and still am, a refugee baby.

As I mentioned, I was made aware of my otherness at an early age. Having transferred to a new school mid-year of first grade, I was already odd man out. Add to that the fact that, while my previous school and neighborhood were racially diverse, I was the only refugee kid that I knew—I just didn't realize it at the time. My new school, however, had quite a few kids from refugee families, most of whom were Vietnamese, with some Chinese, Lao, and Kampuchean kids, as well.

I became fast friends with the other Vietnamese kids, the first I'd ever met that I wasn't related to, due to the fact we all had a special breakout class together, taught by Mr. Liêm, who was himself a refugee. While I had thought this class was to help us learn to read and write in Vietnamese, I found out this was not the case when they eventually kicked me out of the class. I was very upset about this, but I'm not sure if it was because I could no longer attend the class or because this was my first time feeling like an outsider—not only different from others because people are different, but different even from people that are like me.

It turns out that most of the refugee kids at the new school were FOB [fresh off the boat], and what I thought was a Vietnamese language class was actually an ESL class, and since I had come over as a refugee baby six years earlier, I grew up speaking English and Vietnamese concurrently and did not need the ESL class. I never really thought much about that incident, and only a few years ago realized how much it foreshadowed my lifelong inner struggle with self-doubt and yearning for acceptance, to somehow fit in somewhere.

2020 has me revisiting these thoughts and struggles in a completely different light.

Whereas I previously thought that my struggle was to find my place in American society, making the American Dream my own, this year has forced me to take a second look at how I fit in; or, more importantly, whether I should, or even want to, fit in. However, I cannot completely attribute this retrospection to this asterisk year alone, nor entirely to the current White House administration, as I have been contemplating how I self-identify more intensely since I started returning to Viet Nam on a regular basis in 2014. During these visits to my motherland, I have been able to discover and reconnect with a part of myself that was never given a chance to develop, since fleeing from my birthplace meant the abandonment of my Vietnamese self. However, it is also during these visits that I realize how different I am from my "people."

A few years ago, the Vietnamese government allowed former citizens, who had left the country because of the war, to reapply for citizenship. I looked into applying but ran into some bureaucratic obstacles. Additionally, my dad mentioned that it might not be a good idea to have dual citizenship, as I wouldn't want to find myself in a situation where I needed the help of the US government and they refused help, deferring to the Vietnamese government to bail out their native son. It made sense then, and should make sense now; however, with this year and this administration, I can't say that I trust them to have my back. I cannot be true Vietnamese with my American upbringing, and 2020 not only has me questioning what it means to be American, but also questioning how much being American means to me. On top of that, does identifying as Vietnamese-American somehow make me less of both? Thanks, 2020!

Vote "NO to 2020" anytime in the future should these same circumstances present themselves again.

My kitchen didn't used to be this spiteful. Possibly, it has a problem with the windows being taped shut, or with me saying all week, *Today, I'll go food shopping*, or with me poking around her counters and cabinets even though I know the only produce left is an overripe avocado.

It's before dawn and it goes like this.

Five minutes to boil water for my coffee, which is the time it takes to unload the dishwasher, if not for the hundred, lazy, slipshod Tupperware cairns made by whoever emptied the dishwasher last. So, ten. This is the first day of online school and I flash fry breakfast sausage for the kids. An offering. A symbol that says, *Yes, this is fucked up, but it's still school, and I'm still momming you*. While the sausage cooks, I throw in a quick load of laundry. Three minutes, tops. Fling, slam, press start. To save time, I leave the sausage on a plate. Self-serve.

Inefficiency is time stolen. And too much has been stolen already.

My friend who is a writer, who is Black, told me last night that she's done with white women, that she's limiting her output, that she's *on the next plane out*. She means Portland. She means that the literary community has in some way betrayed her. She means it's not one thing, it's everything, and she hates to make everything about race, *except everything comes down to race*. I didn't press the issue, because if she had the energy or the desire, she'd have told me specifically what happened.

Specifically, I'm angry and sad, and I'm making the coffee and sausage and laundry while I sift my brain for anyone and everyone who may have hurt her. I feel my white indignation, which is extra because of the Boston blood in me, but my thoughts are splitting hairs. I respond to her in a video message. My voice catches, my tears rise, but I stand down.

It's not her job to soothe me.

It's post-sausage, pre-avocado, and I stay within earshot of the kids for their first online classes. I'm there to redirect, refresh, and reboot when the internet cuts out, which it will. Nobody has the bandwidth for this. Boy-twins, seventh graders, bleary-eyed at the dining room table, now their classroom. The teen, the sophomore, holed up in her room. I'm in the broken light of the spiteful kitchen, on the listen for YouTubers. Influencers. Sound bites. Filters. Music. I'm listening for open tabs.

But all I hear are the words of a Facebook acquaintance who told me that her relationship with her children was *built on mutual trust*. And that her children need only *a simple conversation about choice and consequence to do what's right,* because *they understand the value of integrity*. Or some such early-on bullshit COVID lecture about limiting screen time and keeping my kids on lockdown for the benefit of others. Left myself vulnerable to that condescending, placenta-munching, no-rules, New-Age who was, by the way, singlehandedly responsible for our school's thriving lice population. I wish I'd written down what she'd said. I want to explode her giant, delusional, self-righteous ego with a stick of cartoon dynamite. *Splat*, all over the desert.

I miss the desert.

I miss rain sky ocean sun hugs. Mouths without masks.

I miss food shopping in a simple N95 mask, not a gas mask contaminated with the searing residue of hexachloroethane.

It goes like this. I reach for the avocado, soft and puckered in its decay, far on its way to disappearing. My nails sink sharp through the green-black skin until I feel its core. Then I split it in two, tear it apart with my finger-claws. The dirty mash of it, seeping over nail and knuckle. Its guts, a sick yellowing, the color of this filthy smoke-filled sky. This smoke disrupts this pandemic disrupts all that we thought we once knew. Life's little disruptions. How we suffer. How we die slowly. Cancer. Emphysema. Loneliness. Or how we die fast. Bullet. Flame. Speeding car. How the lucky ones disappear into their own green-black. Skins shrinking and wrinkling until there's nothing left but Earth's compost. Fire's particulates. Ash on a mantel.

If we're lost in life, maybe in death we are won.

The avocado's skin rips free in pieces. What had once been outside, and what had once been in, no longer matter. They are indistinguishable. The scents and colors of rot bleed together under my nose. This is how it ends. In transference. In stinking clumps. From the whole to the mash. The mystery of my own decay. Of this kitchen's decay.

Are we middle aged? Old aged? Who can tell? We don't know our true timeline until the departing is done.

Transference from my palm to my face. This fruit, this smear of time, covers my mouth, nose, eyelids. In the corners of my eyes. In the crevices of my nostrils. Call it an avocado facial. Call it a psychotic break. Call it cilantro garnish floating down from choking skies. I'm choking. We're all choking. Six days of sealed windows. Box fans with furnace filters taped to their backs. 561: worst air quality on the planet. They're saying *climate change*. They're saying *fix your forests*. They're saying *this is the new normal*. And just before I rub death in my face, there comes another disruption. A small voice, cautious, over my shoulder.

I'm caught. We're all caught. Me, the kitchen, the avocado.

For several seconds, the frame freezes.

"Are you making guacamole?" my son asks.

That is to say, *tell me you're okay, tell me we'll be able to tell time by the sky again soon, tell me you're still here, tell me we are not ripped to the core, we are not on our way to disappearing.*

AMOJA SUMLER

"May you live in interesting times!" You've heard this phrase before. Perhaps you've even said it. Like most "common speech," it's a phrase most of us think we understand without any deeper analysis. What if I told you it isn't a blessing? It isn't even a compliment. It is, in fact, a curse. Interesting times, by definition, need some agent of chaos or else the times would be predictable. Much of language is like this: a seemingly pleasant walk through some simple words, where rhetoric hides in wait, laying traps so subtle as to hardly be deemed a threat. This is the beauty of the insular malice available in the language of the King's speech. English, far from being a neutral arbiter of ideas, is an exceedingly biased and violent language.

I belong to a special class of people who get to write for a living. This is no small thing. Though reading for pleasure is trending downward, we have never lived in a more literate age at any time in history. As such, this allows me an insight into the inner workings of something most of us take for granted: the very construction of the language itself. There are more than 1 million words in the English vocabulary. There are about 170,000 words in common usage, yet the average English speaker only has a working vocabulary of about 20,000 to 30,000 words. Worse, many of the words have wildly divergent meanings based upon the denotative or connotative values. I do not mean to be pedantic. It is this type of attention to language that must be utilized to "say what we mean."

For example: He's green. Look at how much green he has to fold. I see the green in your eyes. He's holding green. The ways in which "green" shifts allow for deeply differing understandings that each phrasing creates. One of the great strengths of English is its ability to do exactly this. Tone can allow for even greater variety when utilized in context. It is something that goes beyond thought. We take it for granted. It's second nature for us to assume all of these meanings are understood as a kind of cultural shorthand. Now, let us examine another color: black.

The official definition for black has 18 entries, of which include: absence of light; soiled or stained; gloomy or pessimistic; deliberately harmful; boding ill, sullen, hostile; without any moral quality or goodness; indicating disgrace or liable to punish; marked by disaster or misfortune; based on the grotesque or morbid; that which is undesirable, substandard, or potentially dangerous; illegal; deliberately false or misleading; or in England proper as slang stands in for "boycotted." In fact, of all the meanings listed in the dictionary, only one has a positive disposition: showing a profit. Consider for a second the irony of "in the black" being a positive phraseology when taking into account the Black Americans' path to the Western world.

Before one even has a solid grasp of racial dynamics, Anglophiles (a fancy phrase for English speakers worldwide) are taught that black is a threat. We could perform the very same exercise on "dark." The reality is, as much as neofascists like Trump attempt to deny it, Western culture in and of itself conditions all of its citizens to embrace anti-blackness as a de facto condition of being civilized. This is only further exacerbated by the Christian dogmatic approach to darkness (akin to the Mark of Cain). A complete irony, considering their seminal head is a father who precedes all creation, who would have existed before time, in the darkness and void of a universe without light. Ironic in *light* of a Lucifer that was known as "the Light Bringer."

English is a fascinating language with built-in devices that allow depth and play. Take for example homophones: words that sound alike but are not. I remember in 2016, Lindsey Graham was a vocal and vociferous opponent to Trump. Then, one day it all changed. Speculation is an unworthy science; however, the scuttlebutt has always been that Graham has secrets, lingering accusations about certain proclivities. The rumors allege Trump discovered some damning proof and has since *blackmailed* him to assure compliance in future agendas. Without even so much as a blink, there we are with a phrase that invokes very strong emotion, sounding phonetically just like an ethnic demographic that makes up about 7% of the American population.

There are huge opportunities for cross-genre research with anthropological and psychological data investigating how these phenomena contribute to the mindstate of law enforcement who act in official capacity as state agents with a monopoly on violence, and its potential to increase an instinct towards violence in relation to Black people. Or rather, there would be ongoing studies if the president of the United States hadn't signed an executive order to de-fund any type of work (scholarly or otherwise) that research causes of racial disharmony that may implicate Western culture itself.

When we think about systemic racism, we tend to think in terms of politicians and parties—sometimes policy for the truly forward thinker. How is it, then, that the very language we utilize is never considered? This is why we must deeply investigate words. Try them out in our mouths. Analyze and dissect them. This is why, though Blacks (with a capital b) may be biased in ways that lead to bigotry, racially speaking prejudiced is a tougher sell, and anti-white racism is not possible. Racism, again a word we take for granted, is not equal to bigotry or prejudice. Racism is equal to bigotry *plus* power.

We live in a world where most Black people are too systemically and economically disadvantaged to even afford a yearly subscription to a service like the Oxford American Dictionary. We certainly have never had the type of societal power to definitively define the official meaning of anything, even down to the intent instilled by the very color of our being. I am a Black man, living in interesting times. In a war with the very language with which I am blessed to make my living.

I ASK, WHAT DOES ONE MORE GRIEF MEAN, TODAY?
LAUREN GILMORE

I sit on a milk crate outside the back door of the restaurant. Snow's settled on the lid of the oil drum. C hugs me against a cold wall, & I ask, what does one more mean—

today?

When M came out to us, no one else in high school knew. He stood in the entryway of the living room like he might walk in, then flicked his wrist like the queens on TV, & said, "discuss."

Before any of us could answer, he turned, walked out the front door & drove home.

I don't remember any of us ever talking about it again.

F's English was perfect, but this made her brow furrow slightly, what does it mean—

to get up from this milk crate? To spill my cup of water across the snow & watch it melt? To read M's obituary? To nod at the inverted sickness of it all, that right now is when we can't have funerals? To count the days when none of us knew, when the world simply folded & cut a hole the size of a person to fall out of?

What does one more secret mean—

today, the snow is melting in patches. C cooks for me. I read Franz Wright's *Earlier Poems* on the couch. I read, *summer is summer remembered*.

What's one more season? What's one more icicle to the bloodstream, bobbing & lifting like it might float? What's one—

year, for my birthday, my family planned a series of instructions for me to find my present. Walk to this room. Go here. Look under this pillow. Each note led to another note. They followed me, laughing, to a basement closet used, vaguely, as a tool shed. I opened the door & M was there, holding a twenty-dollar bill like one of those giant checks on game shows. He jumped out, & I screamed, & what's one more—

note on the way to the center of the bottomless year?

We go down, down the stairs to the tempo of an erratic, conductorless anthem.

Every few paces, another heartbreak, another icicle falling between our feet, sticking straight out of the ground like a dagger that missed. What's one more body, today—

I read, *summer is summer remembered*, & I try not to. What does it mean, now, that I once watched M lift his entire body over the fence at the back of the yard, the one taller than me, to land among the neighbor's raspberry bushes & dodge my water balloon? What's one more trampoline? One photo against the sunset on the prairie? What does it mean—

for memories to turn to sepia in my hands? Now? On my watch? On ours? What does it—

matter, now, that he memorized so many digits of pi? What did it ever? What's one more—

number mean? & what doesn't it mean?
If you kept falling forever—
I mean to ask, what *doesn't* it matter, now—

that all of M's ideas for games involved not seeing:

What if I tell you how to drive the car, & you keep your eyes closed?

What if we're both blindfolded, & have to race to the end of the maze?

No, he said, teaching me how to draw a labyrinth. Do it like this, so they can't see the edges, so every turn comes as abruptly as the last.

In the card game, bury the spoons in the laundry.

In the car, in the dark, in the shrinking room where I wait, rearranging the instructions until they bring us both here, until it's someone's birthday & the snow keeps coming & it isn't cold anymore. An ice cube tray cracking in another room. Every square on the calendar is a shock. I rewrite the instructions. Flip the pages backward, melt.

What does it mean, now? I wait in the ever-expanding room, breathing slow.

"The longer a dead-end, the more it looks like a road."
—Mikhail Turovsky

I sat at my meditation altar on New Year's Eve and pulled an archetype card for 2020. I pulled The Dead End. The circular card portrayed an ominous wall of tangled black branches with a single raised hand in the center. The guidebook by Kim Krans articulated, *"With every bramble, thorn, and stone it simply states, 'No more, child. You have reached the last page of the chapter.'"* It doesn't sound like a promising card, but I wasn't disappointed. I could only assume this new year wouldn't let me continue my ongoing trajectory of overwork and burnout. I had hit the wall many times over the previous two years, but maybe this would finally be the end of the road. I just hoped the worst was already behind me; I hoped the final impasse wouldn't be too brutal, illness-inducing, or world-shattering.

Cross-legged on my round cushion in front of two flickering red candles, I meditated and waited to download the word of the year—what would I return to over and over again? What would be the year's North Star? It came to me quickly: *surrender*. It wasn't what I was expecting, and it wasn't exciting, but I knew it was right. For months, I'd been trying to embrace and integrate the idea that "easy is right." This didn't reflect my normal habits: working multiple jobs, always saying yes, and grinding in New York City and Los Angeles—until starting completely over in a new place. I had always been proud of being unstoppable, but maybe I wanted to be stopped. Why was I always one dental emergency away from ruin? One lost client away from choosing between bills? Why could it never be easy?

My tendency towards workaholism was a combination of necessity, enthusiasm, and habit. I paid rent in the priciest cities without the luxury of a family safety net. I wanted to do a top-notch job in every area all the time, treating small tasks with the urgency of importance. I didn't know how to say no—I wanted the gig, or needed the gig, or both. I didn't know another way. I didn't fit the high-powered, big-city, burnout stereotype, the type who's making bank but is super-stressed and fielding phone calls in her fancy car in LA traffic. I was never the frantic type, or in charge of a prominent firm. I was calm, positive, and the one to lay it all on the line to follow my heart again and again and again. But I was completely burnt out.

It had started one July day in 2017 when I walked in my front door after three clients, burst into tears, and was overcome with nausea. After that turning point, every time I woke up to an alarm and my sleep was interrupted, I felt like I was going to throw up. I'd get dizziness, heart palpitations, and I reluctantly cut out coffee. I saw three doctors who found nothing. The bills kept coming and I couldn't figure out how to scale back, but I decided to apply to graduate programs and go back to school. I needed to change course and leave LA; I needed time; I needed to do something for love and get off survival-autopilot. My increasing numbness and hopelessness scared me. Would I be able to feel joy and creativity again?

The Dead End card suggested a deeper dive by listening to "The Gambler" by Kenny Rogers. *You've got to know when to hold 'em / Know when to fold 'em ... Every gambler knows / that the secret to survivin' / Is knowin' what to throw away / And knowin' what to keep / 'Cause every hand's a winner / And every hand's a loser / And the best that you can hope for / Is to die in your sleep.* Kenny died three months into 2020, at home of natural causes, and, yes, in his sleep. He became an internet meme for bowing out of the year as the pandemic started to become harrowing in the US. Way to know when to fold 'em, champ.

March, the same month Rogers died, I hit a wall again: paid work, full-time school, managing editor of a journal, and the looming realization that I wasn't going to graduate on time despite my breakneck pace. So, I surrendered. For the first time in my life, I backed out of an important work event, a large conference paid for by the university. I couldn't face the thousands of people, long days, and nonstop evening events. The night before I was to fly to Texas, I canceled. That day, San Antonio was declared a city in a "state of emergency" because of COVID-19, and I spent three hours on the phone with airlines trying to ensure a refund. People were starting to panic, but my mind was still occupied by another vicious, growing epidemic: burnout. I wasn't yet sitting at home all day, decompressing and working behind a screen in sweatpants—and my mind-body breakdown was scaring me more than the threat of a new virus.

The next day, I experienced overachiever-relief as I realized hundreds of people had pulled out of the same conference. It was a large and fraught decision for me, but everyone was behaving similarly with last-minute changes—the crisis quickly flattened any ideas about adhering to plans or controlling life. I felt somewhat glad for the peripheral excuse; I felt like my withdrawal could seem less like a personal failing.

I stayed home for a week and didn't leave the house. I was attentive to what was in front of me rather than trying to work and go to class and study and edit and do chores. By the end of my self-created monastic week, the mandatory lockdown started to go into effect. Universities went fully online, restaurants closed. As the seriousness and uncertainty set in, I vigorously cleaned counters, washed my hands, and read Johns Hopkins Center newsletters. But mostly, I felt massive whooshing relief. My friends grieved and lamented having to stay inside instead of going to bars, parties, in-person classes—and I could only think, *Thank you, thank you, thank you for forcing me to stop.*

STACEY Y. CLARK

I n 2020, I found out who I am, and what I am. As social beings, from birth, those around us have filled our heads with ideas about who we are, and what we are. They say, "You're gonna be a doctor," or "You are a concert pianist," or "You're a gymnast," or "You will be a teacher."

They proclaim these things with such certainty that we can't help but take on their visions of our future. Even if only for a little while, we think we know who we are ... what we are. But, what about those of us who have had a vision thrust upon us by delusional parents, finger-shaking teachers, or despondent neighbors that turned out to be more a dream than a vision?

I was informed that I was to be a movie actress. And to my own chagrin, I believed it for too many years. The problem, I thought, was that everyone tells you what you are meant to do, but no one tells you how to do it. There is nothing quite like being filled with a dream when it finally morphs into a nightmare. It's like when champagne's happiness bubbles turn into toilet hugging and acid heaving.

The closest I ever got to being a movie actress was as a background worker, aka extra. Extras are the people you see in the background that make the scene look like real life. They are the folks playing frisbee or chasing their dogs behind the principal actors in a park set love scene. They are the women pressing clothes in the back of the cleaners, the grocery store baggers, the men in hard hats working on the streets, and the waitress taking an order as the stars of the movie walk through life, never even noticing them. And why should they? The movie is not about the extras.

Being an extra is interesting and it turns out it was a metaphor for what my life was meant to be, according to the powers that be; art imitating life, if you will. Extras do not get a script because they have no lines, no words, no voice. Only the principal actors, directors, and technical folks know what is really going on. As a result, extras never know what the story is about or even where the story is headed on any given day of shooting. They are in the movie, and may even be important to the movie, but at the same time, they are menial and not quite members of the cast. At mealtime, they don't eat with the principals or hang out with them, they have their own segregated meals. When they are not in a scene, they are relegated to their own separate space away from the key cast. And once the movie is complete, they are not invited to the party, and they will not see their names in the credits.

For me, March of 2020 was like some high-budget, apocalyptic blockbuster released in time for Spring Break. The surreal storyline was about Black, white, and every other color of human-being taking to the streets of American cities, during COVID-19 (a deadly pandemic), to demand social justice for Black lives. In scene after scene, from city to city, Black and white men stood shoulder to shoulder proclaiming what should have always been known, Black lives matter.

The trailer for the movie, which was in heavy, international rotation, showed a Black man, George Floyd, being murdered, knee-on-the-neck by a white police officer, while other officers looked on. Meanwhile, from the White House, an orange man, the ruthless, powermonger villain type, did everything he could to stop people from caring about one another. All this while emboldened, hate-filled, and domination-fueled white Americans unleashed even more hate than I had ever seen. Black men and Black women continued to be gunned down by the police while the orange man proclaimed there was no systemic racism in America.

2020 was not all guts and gore; there were glorious love scenes. People across cultures, all around the world, displayed more love than I had ever seen in my life; Scots, French, English, and New Zealanders (to name a few) stood up for Black Americans, chanting, "Black lives matter," in their native language, and sometimes dancing. The whole thing made me want to understand more about myself and this place where I live.

I took to researching who I was in America and why so many people were willing to put their lives at risk to ensure that everyone everywhere knew that they believed that my life matters. Why was there ever a question? I needed to know, and what I found has shaken me at my core.

What I discovered was America's script. A script that for centuries only white American lawmakers and politicians (the writers, directors, and principal actors) fully understood. In it, I learned that America is a caste society, dressed up and pretending to be a capitalistic class society, and I am at or below the bottom of the caste because of the color of my skin.

I learned that even on the birthday of America (which ironically is my birthday), I was never meant to be the object of anyone's vision, nor dream, because in this country I was never meant to be a real human, I was never meant to be seen or heard, loved nor happy. I was cast into the background.

Yes, being a Black woman in America is like being an extra on a movie set where I have no voice, little opportunity to emerge, and no place at the party table. This revelation is deeply hurtful. I grew up thinking, if I worked hard, I could be a star.

If only 2020 were just a movie; if only America was not built as a caste; if only the script had never been so cruelly written, and the truth was never revealed on screens around the world.

Now, I know. Now, we all know.

THE FOULEST OF ALL THE FOUL BALLS

JOE AUSTIN

Among all of the many ways that 2020 has fallen short of the once futuristic hopes we'd held for it, for me, none is as swift a kick in the balls as the impact it's had on the sport of baseball.

Once a welcome, albeit occasionally long-winded, distraction, the truncated 2020 season featured fewer total games and a whole host of new rules. I'll stipulate that some of the new rules have been bandied about for years, if not decades, before 2020, but it took a global pandemic to prompt the kind of overhaul wrought upon baseball this season.

I didn't love it when Major League Baseball introduced the two-minute timer a few seasons ago, ostensibly to "speed up the game" (which it hasn't, and who fucking cares anyway?). I've gotten used to the video replay of close plays (though it's baffling to me why, with all of the "cutting edge" tools that we've developed/acquired leading up to 2020, umpires still have to gather around a seemingly Vietnam War-era communication device to confer with MLB's "Replay Operations Center").

To be fair, not all of the new rules are as shitty as 2020 itself. I suspect that the jury's still out when it comes to the long-lasting impact of a Designated Hitter in the National League, or the logic of starting extra innings with the player that made the last inning's final out on second base, and I think it's unlikely that either of those changes would have been absorbed with such little sanctimony if 2020 hadn't already scared the living shit out of baseball fans, who feared that the entire season might be a loss.

As a Padres fan, I've grown accustomed to disappointment. What really chaps my ass is the fact that this just happens to be the year when my 7-year-old son got super into baseball. My third season of coaching his Little League team was cut short by the asshole we call "2020," but the pandemic and resulting months of sheltering in place have resulted in more playing catch and hitting whiffle balls than any two years prior to it. As a result, he has absolutely fallen in love with the game and "our Padres." To put it plainly, 2020 can simply go fuck itself.

I've had season tickets for 23 seasons, and I've patiently sat through some really terrible seasons to get to this one, only to be relegated to watching the games on television and having my son (who's named after Brooks Robinson, for fuck's sake!) pensively ask me, "Dad, if it wasn't for COVID-19, would we be at this game?" I pause, and ponder the innocence and earnestness of his question, and the tears well up in my eyes imagining the added joy of seeing this incredible season through his eyes from the primo seats that I've patiently inched my way into over the past 23 years. "Yes, Brooksie, if this was any other year, we'd be sitting right behind home plate, gorging ourselves on ballpark fare, and cheering our lungs out at the most exciting team in baseball."

There have been so many games this season that have caused me to relive this exchange—like the stretch in late August when the Padres set a major league record by hitting a grand slam in four consecutive games, earning their "Slam Diego" moniker. That was an incredible stretch of games to watch, but my heart sinks every time I see a replay, or see the slogan on a T-shirt or social media post, because we should have been a part of that. It's the kind of touchstone story that my son would have told HIS grandchildren.

Or during the Wild Card round of the playoffs, when Fernando Tatis Jr., a likely National League MVP candidate (one of two on "our Padres") hit not one, but two home runs, to earn a Game 3. Brooksie and I were screaming so loud that I was hoarse for two days—high-fiving like we had hit those home runs ourselves. It would have been a memory that we would have cherished our entire lives, and while I am fairly certain that my son will always be a Padres fan, if we'd been there in person, we'd both have headed straight to a Gaslamp tattoo parlor to make it official. Instead, we brushed our teeth and called it a night.

Adding insult to our baseball season injury, 2020 has also taken a steamy shit on a small business that I've co-owned for 28 years. Live Wire is a small but beloved dive bar (located just a few miles from Petco Park, by the way) which was shuttered on a moment's notice in mid-March, when 2020 kicked its shit show into high gear. I was at the airport in Phoenix with a couple of friends, preparing to board a flight home from Spring Training when the Governor ordered bars (which, let's face it, are a pretty ideal breeding ground for bad decisions) to close.

At the time, we figured it might be a couple of weeks, maybe a month at worst. Here we are, seven months later, our savings nearly depleted, "Shawshanking" crowlers of craft beer and cocktails to our most loyal family of customers and friends each weekend, in an effort to keep our bar's good reputation on the minds of the San Diego community. Even crowler sales are "touch-free"—never mind the fact that we've spent our "down time" improving just about every aspect of our little wunderbar (e.g., greatly improved sound system that no one will hear during curbside crowler hand-offs). Nice work, 2020—you twat.

There are plenty of reasons why 2020 can go fuck itself (see also: "drive-by" birthday parties, Zoom "happy" hours, and gender-reveal-fueled forest fires) but none rises to the level of the double-whammy of losing bars and baseball. My son and I have been robbed of what might otherwise have been the most viscerally awesome, live-and-in-person, baseball-watching of our shared lifetime, and I can't even buy you a drink at my own bar, in person, while I tell you how bad that sucks. None of the other depressingly shitty elements of this year can hold a candle to these offenses to our time with family and friends, and, ironically, the further "our Padres" go in this postseason, the more both will sting.

Yep, 2020 has been a real shit sandwich. Having said that, go Padres!

woke up in a cold sweat this morning from a dream—really, a nightmare—
about Stephen Miller.

You know who he is, right? One of the "senior advisers to the
president," if not the most influential adviser to the president, at least on matters
of immigration. Unlike some of the others (Steve "the other Steve" Bannon
and Roger Stone) who are high-visibility public figures, Stephen Miller keeps
a relatively low profile while he lurks inside the White House with what is
reported as disproportionate access to Trump's ear. He's been called Trump's
surrogate son. It's also been said that Miller is the only one in Trump's inner
circle that Ivanka fears.

But, back to my dream. It is now early in the fall of 2020. The coronavirus
pandemic is raging on with no end in sight. Inexplicably, I'm standing on the
south lawn of the White House where Trump is addressing a mask-less crowd—
all of them, except for me. Literally, every single other person there is gleefully
much closer to each other than the CDC's requisite six feet apart and they are
virtually spitting on each other while they chant, "Four more years! Four more
years!" If that isn't enough to qualify this dream as a nightmare, Miller's well-
known xenophobia is all over the contents of the president's speech, just as his
virus-tainted spittle contaminates the entire front row of sycophants.

I'm horrified—and I'm also frozen in place the way you are in
nightmares—while Trump vilifies everybody from the Chinese "with their
kung flu" to the immigrants who he somehow holds responsible for the financial
crisis. He viciously scapegoats the Black Lives Matter movement and everyone
involved in the protests, starting with Colin Kaepernick and moving on to
name every significant Democratic governor he can remember.

I get a sick feeling as I recognize his rhetoric. It's familiar to me. It's in that moment that I notice Stephen Miller. He's off to the side, skulking behind one of the hedges, and he's smirking. He's smirking at me. He gives a nod to the bloviating Trump and then he signals me with an unmistakable thumbs up gesture. I wouldn't go so far as to say that Stephen Miller looks like a Nazi, but he sure looks like a guy who is trying to look like a Nazi. He also looks very familiar, the kind of familiarity that goes beyond his political celebrity. He winks at me. Then, it hits me. It hits me hard. I know this guy.

Flashback. It's sometime in the early- to mid-aughts. I'm teaching at Cal State, Northridge in Los Angeles. I have just one class. A night class that meets once a week. (Trust me. It's a challenge to engage students who have been working all day and are maybe grabbing some fast food before coming to campus.)

This is an upper division Psych class that is open to every discipline, so, a lot of these students major in Business or Engineering. These majors have little-to-no interest in Psychology in general and even less in my course, "The Psychological Aspects of Parenthood," but Wednesday nights from 7:00 p.m. until 10:00 p.m. fits their schedule. I make an effort to be entertaining. A little song and dance, if you will, to help them stay awake. And I try my best to sneak in some meaningful learning in the process.

About mid-semester, after I have established some rapport and I have enough history with them—a few test scores, some graded essays—I can walk into that classroom of 120 students and, in ten minutes flat, I can create a schism so deep that it has a profound effect on more than a few of them. It is shockingly easy to do, and it can be surprisingly long-lasting. Here's how it works.

By this time in the semester, my students typically like me. I'm not a hard ass, I grade fair, and the course material (human behavior/family function)—once you get beyond their weird fear of being psycho-analyzed—is innately interesting to most of them. I have a sense of humor and, even though I am not by nature authoritarian, the University grants me the authority that accompanies my status as a professor. I, quite literally, have power, albeit a tiny bit, over their grades, if not their lives, to some degree. I am a significant, if temporary, authority figure, for sure. And, through this simple demonstration, I teach them the power of malignant authority. (In this case, I'm concerned with the authority within a family, but the lesson holds true in any organization, large and small.)

So, I usually walk into the classroom and I start a patter in my typical casual style. I'm holding graded quiz scantrons or papers that I pretend I'm going to hand back. I start by saying something like this: "You know, I'm always struck by this phenomenon that happens in every single class that, by now, has become so evident. It's really amazing. I doubt that any of you have heard of this. Maybe one or two of your professors have said something, I don't know. Or it might be an industry secret. It's really startling, though, how true this is."

And they're hooked. A little acting is required.

"Okay, so, I'm going to give you this information so that you can use it to your advantage. It might come in handy for the rest of your school days."

They're waiting. I'm going to give them something. They're alert.

"It has never failed, not once in all the years I've taught, that the people who choose to sit on the left-hand side of the classroom are significantly less intelligent than people who choose to sit on my right."

I am waving their exams at them. *I have proof of this assertion!*

There's a little stir in the room at such a grossly unbelievable falsehood. A few doubt it and laugh. Some overtly scoff. But I keep it up. I intensify the language and I start to make eye contact with the students on my right. I refer to the students on the left as "them." As in, "They are not going to admit this, but you guys know it's the truth, right?"

As I pace in front of the room, I stay mostly to the right. I do what is called "join" with the right-hand side of the room. I move among them. I refer to the people on the right as "us" and "we" and the students on my left as "them" and "they."

"I'm a right-sider. I always have been. Is it because I'm right-handed? I really don't know. How many of you are right-handed? Wow, see? So many are. Maybe it's related to right-handedness." This nonsense goes on for a while. I can take it to the extreme, but, if I do, people on the left at first laugh it off and then start to internalize that they are not aligned with me, the authority figure. It can become painful and I need to be aware that people who have been exposed to this kind of toxic splitting are extremely vulnerable.

Wittingly or not, Donald Trump is an obvious and transparent master of this device, known in social psychology as the "us versus them" heuristic. Using this powerful instrument of division, a toxic authority figure can take any group, large or small, and create schisms so deep and so malignant they are often irreparable. Since his election, and under the white nationalist Stephen Miller's tutelage, we have all watched Trump create unbreachable schisms domestically between the Right versus the Left, Red States versus Blue States, Republicans versus Democrats, and, in 2020, the year of the pandemic, most tragically and fatally for many, the masked versus the mask-less. In the world at large, it is always literally (the) US ... versus CHI-na ... versus NATO ... versus Mexico ... versus immigrants ... versus refugees ... versus shithole nations .... All of THEM out to take advantage of US.

I woke from my dream in a panic, convinced that Stephen Miller had been my student. The timing was right. He would have been in college during those years. He was born and raised in Santa Monica, the suburb of Los Angeles.

Convinced that his thumbs up from the hedgerow beyond Trump was an acknowledgement that he'd learned his lesson in "The Psychological Aspects of Parenthood" well and that he was the mastermind behind Donald Trump's rhetoric. Even now, Miller and Trump are employing the "us versus them" strategy to try to destroy Democracy as surely as they have already destroyed the United States' global reputation as a beacon of hope for those seeking refuge.

Trump used it to politicize the only known deterrent to the spread of the coronavirus that had killed almost a quarter of a million Americans already: the simple mask.

And it was all my fault!

I grabbed my phone. I fumbled for my reading glasses.

"Siri, where did Stephen Miller go to college?" Siri always knows.

"Duke. Stephen Miller attended Duke University."

So, it isn't my fault after all. I would bet good money, however, that there are more than a few Duke professors who are not sleeping well in 2020.

G iven half a chance, and the means, your houseplants would feed off your corpse, no matter how pretty the songs you sing while watering them. The probability that your houseplants would rise up with murderous intent has historically been infinitesimal, but if there were a year it would happen, I'm sure 2020 could fit it in.

From January until now, mid-October, it's been an onslaught of improbable and horrible events, like a checklist for the end of the world. Zombie hurricanes, riots in the streets, secret federal officers kidnapping people in unmarked vans, two wars raging on, a pandemic that may well kill a half a million Americans, and wildfires burning half of Oregon and California at speeds up to 60 miles an hour. By the time this book is published, the election will be decided. Well, nothing is a certainty in 2020, but the election should have been decided. The outcome of this election will decide if we come back from the edge or take off sprinting like lemmings and call the race to our fall "American Greatness."

While there are some immediate unknowns when it comes to the future of our country, democracy, and way of life, there is an obvious truth: no matter who wins the Presidency, no matter if the Senate goes blue or red, the best way to right so many of these wrongs is coming together as a community. I'm going to keep beating this drum: building community is the best way you can fix the world.

I spent my twenty-first birthday fighting in a revolution in Haiti. The people, so poor that they routinely climbed an eight-foot fence lined with razor sharp concertina wire to get into our dump, then they'd fight, and sometimes killed, over the garbage we threw away without a second thought. The downpour of rain in Port au Prince scared me into praying. I had always been agnostic, but seeing that type of extreme weather, weather a sheltered mind didn't think possible, had me talking to God. The water came down so hard and fast, like baptizing the whole island by holding us under to the verge of drowning. I had no idea what I was doing there other than shooting at people who shot at us and walking through the hills for days on end. The only program that I saw make any difference was when we offered to give food for weapons. The people needed food so badly they gave us all their weapons no matter what condition they were in. Some even tried to carve tree branches to look like rifles so they could get a bag of rice. We left, the United Nations came in, Haiti is still struggling.

In Iraq, people I never met or even spoke to before tried to kill me on a daily basis, and they nearly succeeded on more than one occasion. I walked through the rubble of a hospital, a prison, and an industrial complex where no rock bigger than the size of my head remained. One memory still seeds my nightmares weekly: children pouring out of shacks in a makeshift village constructed from rubble to find metal or rock. They survived some sort of firebombing with scars on their torsos, arms, and faces, but the scars and missing limbs didn't stop them from smiling at us, laughing, and being children. I don't know what our mission was there, either. Win hearts and minds by being complete strangers with state-of-the-art weaponry? That was in 2004. The war continues destroying lives and property.

Katrina turned New Orleans into the world's biggest cesspool; a lake with bodies, debris, sewage, and chemicals mixing, floating, saturating. Dogs turned wild, packed at the edge of the seminary we stayed in. If I saw one of them drinking the black floodwater that morning, its carcass would be there that night when we came back. During one patrol, I found a man inside a house with the left side of his head blown out on the drywall of his living room and a revolver still gripped in his right hand. He wore only a pair of white Fruit-of-the-Looms with a piece of white paper plastic-wrapped to his leg. On the paper was his name, date of birth, and social security number. Sometimes, in my dreams, I still feel the fear I imagined was filling him as he wrapped the paper to his thigh, in his dark house, as the deafening hurricane winds beat at the boarded-up windows. We patrolled the streets of the Big Easy with the same weapons, equipment, and mindset we did the streets of Baghdad a year and a half earlier. I do not believe we made a big difference in the recovery of that city.

I found, in all these situations, I was there as an outsider with a rifle in my hand with the mission to somehow help. Help is a very vague term when you don't know anyone by name, you've never met a small business owner, you don't have any investment in helping other than trying to avoid an early death. How could I really help in Haiti, as a young man, when I feared everyone I was there to help? How could I win hearts and minds in Iraq if I can't speak the language and have no idea of the people's history or traditions? Even in New Orleans, in my own country, what was my role or job?

Just living through 2020 means that we've all lived through a time of trauma, but as a special bonus, one of the Oregon wildland fires burned over my community. So, now counting the experiences above, this is my fourth time I lived through the end of the world. The fire burned so fiercely that my family had to evacuate our home for weeks, as did thousands of others. As I write this, over 420 residential and over 30 commercial structures are nothing but ash. Over 200 of those burned homes were uninsured. Over 10,000 trees have been burned and cut down. The landscape will be forever changed. FEMA trucks and other emergency agencies populate the area, and there is no doubt that the fire left us just as destroyed as the streets of Haiti I patrolled during their revolution, the battle fields of Iraq I fought on, or the disaster in New Orleans.

But, on the second day after the fire, we had a group of community members back in the burn area solving problems. I watched people work 12 to 16 hours a day without taking a break for over three weeks. Community members built a relief center that took and sorted donations of food and clothing in the community center. Volunteer EMS and our rural medical staff turned a quilt store into a temporary aid station since our clinic had been burned to the ground. Another, bigger, relief center opened at the K through 12. I watched a handful of unpaid community members do just as much to help an area in a crisis than an army did in times of revolution, war, and the biggest national disaster our country has seen so far. As the county, state, and federal organizations come in, people on the ground, the people who live in the area, are the ones directing what resources would go where and to whom.

I'm not saying we don't need an army. I loved my time in the military and respect the hell out of all who serve, but I will say that our government should look at recruiting and employing people who live in a troubled area to fix that area and its troubles. Give people the means to come together and figure out what they need, as opposed to forcing our way of life on them. Create investment in the people of an area by giving them money and important *and* meaningful roles in the rebuilding process.

On an individual level, we can prepare for disaster by doing some pretty easy things. Learn your neighbors' names, have a beer with them, shop at small businesses, and join a board for a local organization or neighborhood association. If you feel people like you don't have equal representation in the organizations in your community, make a point to join, even if you don't think you have the time. All these things will help you and your community the next time the world ends.

JENNY FORRESTER

I've changed my mind about my friend, Hyperbole.

I was into her in a serious kind of way, sharing her sharp-minded words with other friends and using them against foes.

She said things like, "People die because of you," and "Everyone like you is evil or benefits from it," and "Check your apples," because it's super important to check your apples. Always.

But now, I don't know about her. Hyperbole is all over the political scene in a way I'm not comfortable with anymore. She sounds like a machine, like a Boolean expression of a human being.

She's all, "If [ ], then [ ] else," all the fucking time. You can't just have a conversation with her. She's all, "Everyone who's [ ] is [ ], so [ ]."

She exhausts me. I wish I'd been more up front with my reservations, but now I don't know how to talk to her.

It's too bad.

Hyperbole and I.

We used to have so much fun together.

'd bought the tickets months in advance. Good seats, behind the third base dugout. The flight was booked. Hotel, too.

March 26th of 2020 would have been my 21st New York Mets home opener. It would also mark the 50th consecutive year where I'd been fortunate enough to attend a baseball game in person.

After all these years, for me, it always comes back to that green infield grass. That first glimpse exiting the concourse in search of my seats. Attempting to describe that shade of green is like trying to do justice to an incredible sunset by snapping a photo on your iPhone. You really have to be there.

I didn't get to experience that green back in March of 2020. It was stolen by an insidious thief we know now as COVID-19. Despised yet unseen, an unapologetic menace robbing us of countless loved ones, to say nothing of our sense of community, security, and optimism. The coronavirus targets all that matters most.

But *baseball*? It's only a game. Well, yes, but that's really the point here, isn't it?

It *is* a game, but baseball also happens to be the thread that connects the entirety of my life. For my sixth birthday, Mom and Dad got us tickets to see my first baseball game. I'll never forget that game, or how green the Shea Stadium grass was.

I haven't missed a season since. And over the course of the last 49 years, I've sat in the stands for a game in every ballpark in the country. It's the journey of my lifetime. A journey that appeared destined to come to a screeching halt in 2020, at the hands of the coronavirus.

Baseball in 2020 did eventually return, featuring a shortened schedule and the understanding that all games would be played in empty stadiums. However, things took an unexpected turn when Major League Baseball subsequently announced it had decided to play the 2020 World Series at a neutral site, in front of *a limited number of fans.*

The neutral site would be Globe Life Field in Arlington, the new home of the Texas Rangers. Christened in front of 40,300 empty seats when baseball returned over the summer, Globe Life Field also happened to be *the only ballpark I'd never set foot inside.*

As if we needed more proof that 2020 had a sense of humor, I was scheduled to be in Dallas for meetings on the very dates that Game 1 and Game 2 of the World Series were to be played.

Surely, such an example of cruel and unusual temptation could only be the devious handiwork of the Year 2020. Things were aligned so perfectly that it had to be a setup, one that would undoubtedly end with me having the football pulled away just as I swung my best foot forward.

There *had* to be a catch. Then it occurred to me. COVID-19 was the catch.

In 2020, there was no such thing as a relaxing night at the ballgame. Not with a deadly, contagious virus running amok. Who in their right mind would take on such risk for a *baseball game*?

You bet your ass I went.

And when I caught my first glimpse of the green infield grass at Globe Life Field, I reclaimed a piece of my life.

Fuck you, 2020. And fuck you, COVID-19.

It was time to play ball.

M y eight-year-old and I went to the store for the last time in a long time the weekend before St. Patrick's Day. Already, the cans of beans were gone, and one lone box of Uncle Ben's lay on its side on the rice shelf.

We're vegetarian, so of course we found the lack of beans disturbing. Just kidding, my kid thought it was hilarious.

"They didn't take the good beans!" he said. "They have no idea what they're doing."

Neither did we, but he didn't know that yet. I put on a smile and pointed toward the cans with brown sugar and sauce. Baked beans are like candy. He grabbed four.

We didn't know then how long we'd be inside. So, we filled the cart with three kinds of crackers and five loaves of bread, two bags of corn tortillas and three jars of spaghetti sauce. The flour shelf was bare.

I didn't want to bake anyway. I wanted comfort foods. We only got green beans when we found the mushroom soup too. We could do this.

I repeated it, over and over, *we can do this, we can do this*, as I kicked the wheel of the squeaky cart. *I can do this.*

Still, with each aisle, I could feel something building in me. An ache in my chest.

We rolled the cart on, past bottles of soda and boxes of juice. He grabbed three bags of chips and paper towels. We didn't usually buy paper towels, but the world was dissolving into an uncontrollable virus, and they seemed more sanitary than the dishcloth I tucked into the oven door handle.

I watched them settle into the cart. I had no idea how we were supposed to do this.

My husband's main concern was peanut butter. His texts flashed up across my screen. *Peanut butter. Bread. Beans. Rice. Dishwasher soap. Peanut butter. Flour.* He was setting up his team to work from home, each text more and more urgent. *Hand sanitizer. Dog food. Peanut butter.*

He was out of luck on flour, and the sanitizer was long gone, but they still had the peanut butter he liked. The pull in my chest eased. We could do this. It was just a dozen small steps, over and over again, until we got to the other side.

The shelves of jelly were stripped down.

I swallowed hard.

There were still giant jars of purple goo and unnaturally bright orange marmalade, but the stuff with actual fruit was gone.

I breathed in deep, but the air came in thin. I rubbed my eyes.

"Mom! Don't touch your face. You told me not to."

I nodded my head, wished I could unrub them. How were we going to do this?

We were going to be stuck in the house for weeks, maybe even months, and I could already feel the edges fraying, everything I worked for slipping away.

You see, the thing was, we didn't try on everything, but we tried on some things. Like, maybe no Pop-Tarts or Choco-Whatevers first thing in the morning? Maybe a little protein before a sugar bomb? The baked beans had sugar sauce, but at least they had beans too. Our jelly didn't need to have sugar; it was literally made of fruit.

How were we going to do this?

"Can I get chocolate chips?"

I shook my head, staring at two sad jars of peach jam, all fruit, on the top shelf. *Who ate peach jam?* I checked the date. Still good.

We always got raspberry. But this was a different world, wasn't it? Where the store was out of toilet paper and my son kept making bean jokes and all the jam was gross. We'd have to take what we could get.

I put the jars in the cart and waved away his chocolate chips.

"Okay," I said. "That's enough."

I didn't know there would be another hour in the check-out aisle, and a woman behind us updating her sister about the crazy people with all their masks and hand sanitizer. We couldn't ignore her.

"Are we getting masks?" my son asked. "Don't I have a Spider-Man one? I used to have a Spider-Man one."

Redirect. Refocus.

"Not here," I said. "But do you want to get a magazine?"

We couldn't tell him everything at once, and besides, I didn't even know what everything was yet.

"Do you see any kids' magazines?" I asked.

Two weeks later, my friend dropped off a bag of masks.

"Dump them straight into the wash," she said. "Then iron them again. It takes away some germs and makes them look a little better."

I thanked her, my chest pulling tight. I wished I could hug her, but instead, a soft smile spread across my face.

We don't have what we want, but we have what we need.

I'd explain it to him after breakfast, this whole new world we were living in, with face masks and sanitizer and peach jam.

I pulled the toast out of the toaster, and he spread the jam. He ate his breakfast with sticky fingers.

E very empire decays and falls. When the elders are no longer pillars of the community, but craven, twisted shadows of their fathers; when the holy places have all been desecrated and academe curdles in the high places; when the police wantonly commit murder in the streets; then, what has come before must not have been respectful!

We were wrong to ever think our institutions strong or wise, or to assume there would be respite and solace for the poor and working classes, or to believe in anything like mercy or forgiveness. We have always been wrong to tarry in drinking halls, fawn in the shadows that avarice casts, to indulge our base desires more each decade.

The way we forget is all wrong. Somehow, as Americans, we remember the worst kernels of truth and wrap them in fictions so vicious and untoward that they invite our belief. We've forgotten all the lessons of Operation Wetback in the '50s, when we sent Mexicans back across the border to Mexico after their usefulness came to an end, and everything we could have learned from MK-Ultra, little more than rumor lost in conspiracy's murmur. And then Vietnam happened, the civil rights movement, and on and on and on. So, don't be surprised when people scream and rave when betrayed.

There will be nowhere to hide when the scorn of our children rises up to cast us down and out, nowhere to run when the acolytes of the new order have had enough. We saw a little of that happen with Eric Parker on a ridge overlooking a gulch during the Bundy standoff, and even more of it happened in the streets in pink pussycat hats, or beneath red and black standards. Soon enough, we'll hear them coming up the street, for us this time.

And if our nation's great union proves untrue, then we must undo it.

T he racehorse figurine next to a one-eyed Daruma doll reminds me that it's time to sit down and work. The doll will be forever blind in one eye if intentions don't become realities. The horse, a gift from an intern I helped, will be forever frozen in stride if the next turn never reveals a finish line.

My sadness eats away at intention. A bite. A bite. A bite. Little thoughts come to mind while I settle into my chair. Doubts. Admonitions. Fears.

The outside air has covered the world in haze, and the radio warns that fires rage and air quality is the worst on record. By the time I have turned on my computer for a meeting, the radio has shifted its electron flicker attention to the deaths of thousands and attacks on government fools who ignore science.

For a moment, the voices die back. For a moment, I think I might pick up my N95 mask and wear it during the meeting to make the point that I, at least, am aware of the need for safety.

I do not. The electrons slip and slide, forever in motion and never arriving, or arriving but impossible to find. The voice reminds me that my job is like the electrons, tenuous at best. I fear for myself and my family because I know the manager who runs this meeting is one of *them*, those people who are so sure that they know things that they don't have to bother checking what they believe against any standard other than themselves. An idea came to them; therefore, the idea must be true.

My ten-year-old comes into my office while the computer finishes an update and boots. She shows me a math problem. She's in class on her laptop in her bedroom, and it makes me a little uncomfortable that her bedroom is on anyone's screen outside our family, but we have cleaned it. We set up her desk and workspace. We all agreed it was for the best.

The problem is simple enough for me, an engineer with ten years on the job, but teaching is not so easy. I help her work through the concept and apply it to the problem.

She's happy. She bounces back to her classroom.

I turn to my screen and see the Zoom link pop up from my calendar.

A couple clicks, and a series of news popups appear, as they do every morning: debate bullying; White House afflicted by pandemic infections; global deaths; American deaths lead the world; economic downturn; businesses closing; collusion; resignations; indictments; dirt from the past; and a die-off of fish in Alaska where acidic water has poured into the rivers after leaching through soil that has thawed after being frozen for 12,000 years.

The meeting pops up its *Hollywood Squares* format. The team appears, one head at a time.

I reach to flick off the radio. The last words I hear are, "... future generations."

I need the job. We need the job.

I reach for the mask and put it on, knowing it's pointless. It's a futile, useless protest gesture that will cost me and my family.

Everyone is in the meeting. A couple people comment. My friend and partner on the project, Zaille, puts on their mask. Paul, an attorney, suggests it's not necessary and might be inflammatory, but Pamela, who will likely lose her job when her child is born, nods and puts on hers.

Several others seem to understand. They have masks at hand and put them on.

The manager of the project is late.

Seven people out of fifteen have masks on before the manager's admin pops up. "He is in the hospital with COVID," the young man says. "We're asking for prayers for him."

Someone laughs, but nobody knows who because of the masks.

The team gets more done in the meeting than any previous meeting and, by the end, twelve wear masks, including the attorney Paul.

When the meeting ends, I smile at the horse and the one-eyed doll. The project isn't done, but it will be. The Daruma doll will see again. The horse will finish.

I make a donation to a PAC in support of the Green New Deal, and then go to check on her math.

NOVEMBER 2020

NOVEMBER 2 – Trump: "Joe Biden is promising to delay the vaccine and turn America into a prison state—locking you in your home while letting far-left rioters roam free. The Biden Lockdown will mean no school, no graduations, no weddings, no Thanksgiving, no Christmas, no Fourth of July."

NOVEMBER 3 – Election Day

NOVEMBER 4 – US reports unprecedented 100,000 cases in one day.

NOVEMBER 7 – At 11:25 a.m. EST, 8:25 a.m. PST, Biden is named President-Elect.

NOVEMBER 7 – Kamala Harris is the first woman and first person of color to be elected Vice President of the United States. Her husband, Doug Emhoff, is to become the first Second Gentleman and the first Jewish spouse of a U.S. Vice President.

NOVEMBER 9 – President-Elect Biden announces COVID-19 Transition Team.

NOVEMBER 9 – Pfizer publishes vaccine results.

NOVEMBER 16 – Moderna reveals vaccine efficacy results.

NOVEMBER 24 – Elon Musk overtakes Bill Gates to become the second richest person in the world, with a net worth of $127.9 billion, behind only Jeff Bezos.

277,461 DEATHS | 14,020,115 INFECTED

n 2003, *The Zombie Survival Guide* came out. I was 16. A year later, my too-cool-for-me, gothed-out friends invited me to join their text-based fantasy zombie apocalypse dream team. I declined. I'd seen the movies. Though I didn't have a name for it then, I knew what I was: the magical morale booster with no "real skills." You know, the one who cracks jokes or lopsidedly romances one of the leads? The one who's killed. Usually at the end of the second act, at a moment when everyone thought things might be okay, almost always gruesomely, perhaps with a slow-mo shot (equal parts my demise and the distraught faces of survivors). The ostentatious brutality of my death bringing the group low with an excruciating thump. But then, also, somehow being the catalyst for their last stand and ultimate victory.

I didn't know I was queer at the time. I didn't know I was trans. But I knew I was some kind of expendable. Not just that I was expendable, but that in the event of an emergency, my body and my emotional sincerity were to be appropriately, even beautifully sacrificed for "those more capable." It's not that I wasn't tough. I was. (I am.) But I was also so fucking swishy. And that could not be quashed to express even an ounce more of my tough. All the narratives of apocalypse and horror that I encountered reliably, unequivocally served up characters displaying any such qualities a horrifically manicured death sentence.

In the years following my first puberty, I reveled in this narrative of myself. Fetishized it. Beat off to it, even. It gave me meaning and value in society's eyes. The fact that it required my death wasn't much of a problem. To be honest, I kinda found it hot (too). With my empathy extended, I became deeply moved by my own demise.

You younger whippersnappers must understand, talk of the zombie apocalypse was all the rage throughout the entirety of the 2000s. Our end-of-the-world weapon of choice was what we talked about on first dates. (Gawd, remember first dates?) It was what we posted on our first OkCupid profiles (mine was a machete). It was how we got through eight years of George W. Bush. When the reality of apocalypse is hidden from sight, people get imaginative, I guess (Dick Cheney was more of an illusionist than anyone Trump's ever jammed into/ejected from his cabinet).

In George A. Romero's iconic *Night of the Living Dead*, Ben, the competent, clever, sexy-as-fuck, Black protagonist is, at the end of the film, shot dead by a well-armed militia of white men. They do this from a distance assuming he was a zombie (too). Despite Romero's claims to colorblind casting, I know I wasn't the only one absorbing certain narrative elements about who gets to survive the apocalypse and why.

My point here is that, in fantasy versions of the apocalypse, the people who are sacrificed to those narratives and how they are killed can be instructive. Not of how the *actual* apocalypse might go down, but of how those who've never been to the apocalypse imagine they might be able to survive it: by the courtesy deaths of those who aren't white, or able-bodied, or cis, or straight, or well-resourced. Of course. It's not really so surprising. Same old, same old. It's just that you can see the blood and guts in these versions.

I think part of being oppressed is being made to carry a sense of the apocalypse inside of you always. This can be/has been administered through physical and systemic violence, like chattel slavery, prisons, conversion camps, and the internment, forced removal, and torture of peoples deemed threats to the state. Etc. (So much etc.) This sense of apocalypse can also be administered, inherited, and internalized more quietly, but regularly, and just as systematically. So, maybe the apocalypse is actually just colonialism? This is not five-paragraph essay. That's not my thing. I'll tell you once what I wanna tell you. After that, it's up to you to tell yourself any version you want. But I think a therapist might call the apocalypses I'm talking about "trauma." I'm not a therapist, but I've seen a few.

And, having seen a few, I know that one of my reactions to the apocalypse inside me is a dour, grinding, Eeyore-esque anxiety sourced from a certainty that the worst is always likely to happen. I don't know where it came from, but it's been there since I was a child. These days, I'm well aware of the people and forces in this world who wish I didn't exist or existed less (loudly). Often, I project onto others and their small slights of me this self-annihilating hex. I panic and I rage in reaction to small irritations as if they might be trying to kill me. Remember, my death has been inevitable from the beginning of this horror story? I have envisioned it many times. (And it's so hot, amirite?)

During "good times," I am so scared of the worst happening, I can barely move. My own success paralyzes me. When the "bad thing" happens, my body is always ready for that contingency. I move with purpose and efficacy. When my spouse threw me out of our house, I felt shock but also relief. I looked up at the sky and bellowed, "I told you so!" Three months later when the 2016 election results came down, in what was, for some people, the worst night of their lives, I felt the same way. Hollowed out and ready. Here it is. My time to be of use.

The thing is, those zombie movies were wrong. Being the morale booster, the magical fairy gaymother who can get someone tea when they are immobilized by their apocalypse IS invaluable. Being an entity whose art, and friendship, and romance involve loving others with maximum vulnerability and truth, that's what it actually takes to survive and even live well at the end of all things.

2020 has not been the worst year of my life. In fact, I've never wanted to be more alive. Never been surer of my survival. Never been surer of my purpose and worth. It's kinda fucked up to say so, but 2020 has been a great year for me. People's sense of mutual aid and justice are expanding and activating in my communities like never before. (I know it's in response to crises, but witnessing it feels good and a long time coming.) I'm eligible for more government services and community grants than ever before. More than ever before, when I have had extra resources this year, I've felt okay sharing that, despite an uncertain future. I no longer feel like such a fucking edge case. Feels like all of the struggles are being exposed. Suddenly, I'm not so alone anymore. We are living together and dying together.

Almost all of what I have been scared about my entire life, the thousands of brutally sacrificial deaths and murders I've envisioned for myself aren't happening. And this apocalypse-via-pandemic is NOTHING like any of those zombie apocalypse stories. There are no singular saviors, no clear Strong Silent Leaders. The saving, when we can manage to save each other, is happening between tired hands and hearts, in the streets and in the swelling of bail funds. The saving is us working to divest from transaction, a passing back and forth of what little is available at a given time; a shared knowing that it's far too little, and then sharing anyway. It's abundance with minimum ownership, actions with maximum ownership.

When my part-time job folded in August, I took a few breaths and leapt. I've taken what little money I saved up in my scared time and moved into my own apartment. It has enough space for a small office. I'm now focusing full time on writing, teaching, and performing. Who knows if it will work out. But it's the end of the world. I've been preparing for this my whole life. The apocalypse is my inheritance. It's flush with brutally beautiful truths that the old narratives could never contain.

I know I said that I wouldn't have a thesis, but I gotta say it straight as I can (y'know, in case there's any straights in the audience): When you talk about this hell year like it's the first time, remember that the apocalypse has been here a long time, gruesomely playing itself out on the inside and outside of oppressed bodies the world over. And they're the ones, with all that apocalypse experience, who are getting the world through this. So, if you got resources to spare, I suggest you pay your dues and fund the abundance of the experts here.

Oh, and one final note: It took me a long time to realize this, but envisioning a future, any type of future, wherein you die, or where there's no place for you to live, is a kind of suicidal ideation. I'm not saying don't get kinky with the brutality you were dealt (by all means, DO). I just want you to remember to take care of yourself and know that there are people who *do* believe in a future where you live, a future with space for all your multitudes. I know I do.

DeMISTY D. BELLINGER

On March 10, 2020, the day was warm for New England. Blaring alerts from the university where I work light up my phone and laptop: "Extended spring break." I'm in a spacious coffee shop with a friend and my husband. It's Hollywood sunny, the type of light where something feels off, and the stars believe they're in the clear, but they're not. When we get the alerts, I cringe. Remember the scene in *Bonnie and Clyde* when Beatty and Dunaway's characters meet their end? It's in dandelion-colored sunlight. That's the color of the day when we learn the governor has declared a state of emergency. We learn, too, the potential of danger to us.

I feel the same shock and hurt as being punched in the face. As a kid, I fought a lot, and I experienced it firsthand many times. A sudden, physical sting. Or is the sting I feel, when I learn our worlds will change, more like falling down? Again, as a kid, I scraped enough skin from my knees and the heels of my hands to know that sting. That pain, too, is sudden.

Sudden: I avoid that word in my writing. Nothing in life happens suddenly. In creative writing classes, I gently steer students away from that word. It's a lazy transition: something had to happen to build to that point. Life is all about causes and effects, not sudden changes.

But in less than a minute, the world shifts.

It happens suddenly.

Life becomes a bad television show; or worse, I am a product of dramatic irony.

I teach my students about this literary device. But they are undergrads and haven't perfected it yet. It's difficult to balance ignorance and knowledge when you have control over all information.

We're told that not only has the virus made it stateside, but it has infiltrated the Commonwealth of Massachusetts. It took root in our nursing homes and spread itself indiscriminately at a conference for, of all things, a biotech company. If these were plot points in a student's post-apocalyptic fiction, I would deftly interrupt the praise or constructive critiques from their peers and tell them that, though I enjoy the knowledge of the attendees at the biotech conference who all stand around and speculate on the novel coronavirus out of a previously little-known Chinese province (little-known from Americans, that is), the irony seems too forced. Why not make it another kind of conference? No, not a writers' conference. That, too, would be too convenient.

And I would point out that the greedy politician is clichéd. This character is right from the *Jaws* playbook. Yet here we are: a president who wants people not to worry and to shop instead. Governors and mayors who want their towns open. Members of Congress and senators questioning science. I would have explained the concept (probably again) of suspending disbelief and how the audience will no longer be able to suspend it. People will question the logic of the story.

A good story is more than a good story: it is at least two good stories. A short story, novel, TV episode, or movie should have at least two stories moving in tandem. Characters, too, should be multifaceted. This is what I teach. I tell my students that there are main plots, and there are subplots. But the subplot can't be as strong as the main plot. And the three-dimensional character must have one strong trait.

This coronavirus story isn't working that way. I, as a character, have guilt competing with anxiety. My love of family is rubbing against my hate of national politicians. My will to survive a pandemic is grappling with my exhaustion of living in a pandemic.

And the subplot is competing with, if not superseding, the main plot. Breonna Taylor was killed in her home. Police officers with a no-knock warrant storm into her Kentucky apartment and shoot her to death. Taylor, an EMT who dreamt of being a nurse, is shot to death. Taylor, another black woman committing no crime, dead at the hands of police officers who fail to see that her life matters. That is in March.

In May, Minneapolis cop Derek Chauvin knelt on George Perry Floyd Jr.'s neck for nearly nine minutes. This brutal act towards an unarmed man is accompanied by bystanders telling Chauvin to stop, but he continues to kneel on Floyd's neck. Chauvin fails to see that Floyd's life matters.

While we wipe down surfaces with alcohol and disinfectant; while we watch loved ones get sick and/or die from an ugly disease; while first responders deal with the dying, frustrated with the inability to help; while frontline workers continue to get sub-living wages to ring up our groceries and bag our food, and put their lives on the line; while hundreds of thousands of Americans lose their jobs to COVID, then their homes, and their family members, police officers in Kentucky and Minnesota decide that they are above the law. They decide black lives are expendable. Not only do we have to deal with the disproportionate number of black and brown people in America (and really, it is in America; most of the African continent is doing well with suppressing the disease) losing their lives and livelihoods to COVID-19, we have to deal with the disproportionate number of black and brown people being abused and dying at the hands of American cops. Why wouldn't people take to the streets, masked up and armed with protest signs, and demand justice?

The deaths of fellow Black Americans and the subsequent protests leave me beyond worried. Shaking. Eye twitching. Were this a student's story, I'd write marginalia about this being too much for the protagonist. "She isn't Job," I'd say. "She can't suffer this much." I'd tell the student, "These two events—this pandemic and this police brutality—are equally horrible. What is your main conflict?"

And let's say the third subplot is that the president has compromised the post office. Then, because the student didn't feel like enough is going on, he kills off one of the most reasonable and powerful women characters, a Supreme Court justice holding back the tyranny of fundamentalism. I'd have to invite that student to my office hours. We would have a conversation that may get uncomfortable. I would ask, "What is going on? What is happening in real life that inspires this story?" Then, we'd work on a revision plan.

But this is not a story; it is what we're living. Reality sanctions absurdity; these times are stranger than any I've ever experienced. This onslaught of horrible events is a sudden fist to the face. It's not that sudden, though. We quickly learn about lots of lead-up to this moment. The Trump Administration ignored the Obama Administration's warnings regarding a potential pandemic. John Bolton disbanded the pandemic task force, the Directorate of Global Health Security and Biodefense, by encouraging some members of that unit to resign and reassigning others to different departments. The Trump administration still poo-poos the infectious disease scientists and prefers to present a rose-colored world.

And as the worst thing in the world happens, another worst thing in the world happens. Again. The disregard of Black lives is an ongoing reality in the United States. This uprising is long overdue, but similar protests happened before; I am certain they will happen again.

I hate the saying "stranger than fiction," but I feel like we're living in times that are, indeed, stranger. My face stings, or my mind, or maybe it's the pressure of the masks. Still, reading reality like a draft in progress helps me cope with the ridiculousness of this reality. I address the real world not so much as bad writing, but as work by an aspiring writer.

COVID-19 thrusts us into this story. If this was a student's work, I'd tell them that they should have ended it earlier. "Maybe these people deserve a happy ending," I would say, "or something happier. How would that look?"

PHOTO:

TWO ANTS

CRAWLING ON A FADING

CAMELLIA BLOOM

TEXT: There's always been enough time to watch ants, but only if watching ants was important enough. Now we get to remember—watching ants is always important enough.

I. SEPTEMBER 2019

The ceremony of my first meditation retreat felt incredibly uncomfortable. The bowing, the bells, the snarling deities that hung on the wall. Apparently, the cynical dismissal of ceremony and ritual I'd adopted as a teenager had softened over the decades but hadn't completely worn off.

Six of the hospice patients I provided massage for had died in the two weeks prior. It's hospice. Death is in the job description. But as a massage therapist with a small case load, it was heartbreaking to have more than half the people I visited die so close together. During almost every meditation, a soreness bloomed inside my chest and I often cried.

During almost every break, I found my body demanding ritual even though I didn't really know what ritual meant. I'd sit on a low rock in the high desert sun and find an ant. Then I'd follow it along its path to discern how the obstacle of a stone, a footprint, or a tangle of hair would alter its route. I didn't think the ants held the spirits of Joan, Murray, Esther, and the rest, but I didn't NOT think the ants held their spirits.

I didn't know what spirit meant anyway. I didn't know what death meant either.

PHOTO:

gray sky

ABOVE THE
TIPS
OF BARE

FORSYTHIA BRANCHES

TEXT: I've always done this—put a frame around the world so that just the beautiful thing remains. I used to do it as a kid, narrowing my focus down on a raindrop on the car window or a flower in a median strip .... So, today, in the fifth hour of steady rain, I look past the rooftop of the giant, gentrifying house and find some worthy silhouettes waving in the stormy sky.

II. JANUARY 2020

At first, it was just a project, a way to start writing again and bring more focus to the urban nature pics I'd been posting. I'd frame each day of 2020 with a photo and a few minutes of free writing. Nothing precious. I'd use my phone for all of it and post the results while still lying in bed each morning. I'd use my eyes and fingertips and the clenched spot in my chest that hadn't gone away. I knew there was no making sense of it all, only a pointing, a presenting.

Here. This.

That felt like enough. Though I didn't really know what enough meant.

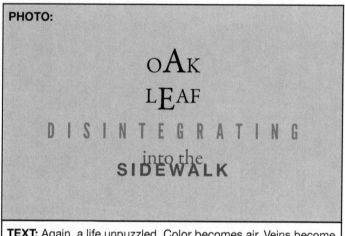

PHOTO:

oAk lEAf DISINTEGRATING into the SIDEWALK

TEXT: Again, a life unpuzzled. Color becomes air. Veins become skeletons, undone bone by bone. What a relief.

III. MARCH 2020

Maybe I'd grown used to death being framed inside the routines of hospice care, forgetting that sometimes the end arrives without anyone there to gently usher it in. On March 11th, I was dismayed when I received my notice: "Access denied due to COVID precautions." No more massage. To all my beloved clients I became threat instead of tenderness, harm instead of relief. I was asked to stay home, like their sons and daughters, and watch the world try to wrap itself in safety as the dying carried on their work without us.

Sheltered at home, my body returned to ritual. By now, I had a shrine set up in a corner of my house, though I shunned the buddha statues and Tibetan thangkas that accompanied the lineage I'd been studying meditation under. I gave up on the chants, aspirations, and dedications that came with the lineage too. Then, the organization's head teacher followed a sadly familiar path of harm and denial, and I gave up the lineage altogether.

No matter. I knew my body had to make its own way through this, around stones, footprints, and tangles of hair. My body had to sink into a practice that became part prayer, part pause, part deep body dive. A ritual of silence and smoke tree blossoms. A ritual of paper inscribed with the names of the dead and burned down to ash.

And I knew even less what death meant. I knew less and less about more and more all the time.

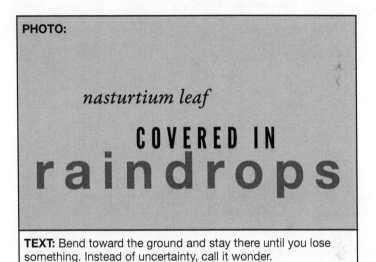

PHOTO:

nasturtium leaf

COVERED IN

raindrops

TEXT: Bend toward the ground and stay there until you lose something. Instead of uncertainty, call it wonder.

IV. APRIL 2020 – PRESENT

My walks to photograph the cycles of neighborhood gardens or some unnoticed curve of metal and moss have taken on more weight than I ever intended. Weaving my way through the streets and aiming my camera at some small enticement has become entertainment, distraction, exercise, and practice all in one.

I find that, for those few early morning minutes of pairing word with image, clarity is not required. The ritual is an invitation to sit confused inside the silt stirred up by the world. To sit with the virus, the racial inequities, the unhoused humans, the fire that raged in my neighbor's home and in the streets of my city and in all my favorite forests, the raging political divides, and all the deaths both close to home and far away.

The ritual asks me to sit inside the familiar pinch behind my rib and sternum. And adore dying flowers. And take advice from trees. And abandon answers. The ritual asks me to not urge the silt to settle. Things are going to be kicked up for a while. This is not only okay. This is everything.

This is my body moving toward a more awkward place. And I no longer know the difference between awkward and right.

PHOTO: *fall foliage on a **dark** green* F O R E S T   T R A I L

TEXT: The morning rose surprisingly gentle. Nothing more to do. Or rather, calm is my job now. Slow is my work. Two months ago, this forest was thick with smoke and red with approaching fire. But the waterfall still spilled, and the river still flowed, and the rocks beneath them grew a little smoother.

The jacket of smoke said it all. I was sitting in the lounge of the detox unit, pretending to watch the television—all the while counting regrets—when that helpless koala galumphed towards animal rescue, smoke trailing from its fur. The smoldering soul, no longer concerned by the threat of a stranger, climbed into the man's arms not unlike the way I surrendered at intake, "Whatever I have to do, I'll do. Just don't turn me away."

I was seventeen days without alcohol. Seventeen days without heroin or crack. Christmas decorations were still nailed to many walls. Images of the damage I'd done, nailed to the inside of my skull.

"Hey, Mr. Blake. How are you?" Kevin was the friendliest counselor in the place, although I could tell by his tone, he asks that question at least one hundred times a day.

"It's day 17, Kevin."

"So, wha's that mean?"

"That means that's all I fucking know. I'm clean and sober 17 fuckin' days." I glared at him.

Kevin's smile stretched from ear to ear. "That means ..." as he leaned down, "you're still alive."

"You say that like it's something to celebrate."

Kevin laughed at my response. His Jerry Garcia tie jiggled above his belly. He was the only staff member that refused to be intimidated by me—most likely because he was the only person just as big as me. He turned to look at the television, "Is that a koala on fire?"

"It's smoldering. Most likely got burns somewhere. And you know what?"

"Wha's that, Mr. Blake?"

"I know *exactly* how that poor bastard feels." Tears welled up, and Kevin told me to stand. I stood, and this bear of a man became Animal Rescue, his embrace was a cool, soft towel, smothering all my smoke, chasing all the wraiths away.

I had never been to a rehab before. I'd gotten clean a plethora of times, but never allowed myself the opportunity to be still at a facility for months while I learned about the chemistry of my brain and why my thinking had been out to kill me. I learned a great deal about Post-Acute Withdrawal Syndrome. I began to understand how the perfect storm of trauma, mental illness, and chemical dependency—experienced by both my parents and their parents—had everything to do with where I was standing and how I'd gotten there.

Every morning, Kevin greeted me, "How many, Blake?"

"18 days," in a low growl mixed with cynicism.

"26 days," with a shrug of my shoulders.

"42 days," and a sincere smile.

"66 days," as the tears rolled.

"What's going on?" Kevin asked.

"Kev, I just wanna die, man." And he crushed my pain in his arms while I soaked his shoulder. I could feel the smoke rising from my skin. It was as if my entire life had been burning, and using was all I could do to endure the scorch. No matter how long I managed to stay sober, depression prevented me from enjoying my successes, big or small.

I sat with Kevin and two other therapists at the facility. I began to tell them everything: the sexual assault I endured at 16; the day my father was thrown out by my mother when I was three; the night my mother was dragged away by police; even the moment I discovered my oldest brother died from hypothermia. I recalled the moment my mother took her last breath—three days after she decisively overdosed on her insulin. All around me were flames.

I started taking antidepressants for the first time in my life. They actually began to work. Kevin also suggested I write small gratitude lists to begin my day; just five things I am grateful for every morning.

"How long, Mr. Blake?"

"80 days, Kev," and we laughed together.

Sometimes Kevin would bring up, usually around other clients who just arrived that week, "Man, you wanna know miserable? This guy! Man, the first day I met him, I said, 'How are you, sir?' and he said, 'I'm three days sober, I'm fuckin' detoxin'! How the fuck you think I'm doing?' And what is it now, Blake?"

"Day 80."

"And do you feel any better?"

"Oh, fuck yeah."

Then, other clients would begin to talk to me about being clean, and giving the staff a shot, and helping them try something new. We'd talk about EMDR, DBT, and groups that covered various topics of sobriety.

Two clients that stood out were Ryan and Bailey. Ryan was a skittish, anxiety-laden 18-year-old from North Carolina. Bailey was a rebellious 20-year-old spitfire from Virginia. Ryan didn't think being clean was possible. Bailey had no interest in trying.

One night, Ryan found out his grandfather died, and his parents wouldn't agree to Ryan going home for the funeral. He sobbed uncontrollably. Fellow clients came to my room to get me. I was the only option to calm Ryan down. He and I talked about the word "coincidence." I asked him what he would have done if he were home when he received such news. He said he'd use.

"Well," I said, "that's why you found out in here."

By the end of our talk, Ryan was feeling more settled and vowed to stay clean for "Grandpa."

Bailey thought getting or staying clean was for fools. "There's nothing about this world worth being clean for. Nothing!"

Bailey lost her father to bullets and her closest aunt to an overdose. The boyfriend she hooked up with at the facility snuck off campus, bought booze, and came back drunk. He was released and sent to another facility. I shared with Bailey my own torments; those I've lost, I've hurt, and the many chances I've had to do better but failed. She because a daughter of sorts to me.

Over time, other clients became siblings. Gatherings became sweet blends of cigarette smoke and sanguine emotions. We laughed, trading stories of toxic family, physical abuse, and well-executed lies we told to escape jail or worse. Sometimes, someone would share a tale of abandonment or grief. We were there for each other. I can't remember how many times someone from the facility cameoed on my morning gratitude list. My day couldn't start without trying to drag Ryan to sunrise yoga, and my day never ended without cigarette time with Bailey.

5:00 a.m., day 86, I put my bags in a transport van, and headed to the airport. Ryan was still in bed, but Bailey, with a face full of tears, grabbed one of my bags and escorted me to the van. We hugged numerous times. I told her how absolutely proud of her I was. She was clean over a month, working honestly with her therapist, and attending all groups. She even began to lead an evening group and open up to many women there. People were looking up to her. I knew that both Ryan and Bailey had futures ahead of them, glinting with more promise than my younger years. I was grateful for the opportunity to play a small role in their new lives.

En route to the airport, I had the same driver that picked me up to take me to rehab. He looked at me through the rearview mirror and smiled, "And they said it can't be done. People say it's impossible for us to get and stay clean, but here you are. How long are you sober, John?"

I took a deep breath, and in a sigh of relief I responded, "eighty-six-motherfucking days," and we both cracked up.

On the way to rehab, I remember him asking me if I was okay. I couldn't stop sobbing. "I don't know if I can do this, man. I just don't know if I got it in me to get clean again."

"Look out that window to your right. Look up." It was a large, Navajo-white moon. "With a moon like that, and a God that must have made it—how could a God like that not give you the strength to do this one more time?" I didn't believe in God, but I did stop crying. I stopped shaking, for the most part.

I got to the airport with just enough time to make my flight. I forced myself to find some sort of comfort in order to sleep on the plane. I didn't want to be awake. I didn't want to have any opportunity to answer the flight attendant when they asked about beverages. I was afraid of my answer.

I made it to my new city, Albuquerque, New Mexico. My friend was there to drive me to my new home. I was in New Mexico two days—meditating, attending meetings, and even secured employment. Korbin was the first addict in recovery I met when I got to Albuquerque. We reached out to each other from time to time. He was not yet thirty. We'd talk about love and relationships, women and manhood, fatherhood and our parents. I was grateful to have someone to bond with, grateful for my new friendship.

Suddenly, not even two days thriving in my new city, the announcement came that the state would be shutting down for quarantine to reduce the spread of COVID-19. My job shut down, and all residents were strongly urged to remain in their homes.

After two weeks of staying home, alternating between bare walls and a laptop screen, I found myself outside, smoking cigarettes and looking up at the sky. Some nights, I stayed out in the backyard, stargazing, until, behind the mountains to the east, Albuquerque's sunrise would commence. When the sunrise began, I wrote a short gratitude list; five things I was grateful for. I was coming to terms with my gender identity, which seemed to constantly queer itself more and more. I journaled about my transformations. I contemplated on the courage it took in rehab, after discussing my new expressions with my therapist. I considered how desperate my spirit must have been when, in an all-men's group, I voiced my need to wear more feminine attire, mascara, and eyeliner, and, to my shock, many men not only stood up for me, but hugged me in support. There is something about a sunrise hiking over mountains that must be seen.

I kept in touch with my rehab family. We checked in with the group daily, until people stopped checking in. Jon relapsed first. We knew because he started texting all of us for money. Then, Elaine. She just dropped off. Susan came out as bisexual in rehab, and her biggest fear was telling her family. She never told them. Instead, as soon as her plane landed from rehab, she went straight to the liquor store to secure her secret. The hardest hit was Ryan. He and his girlfriend broke up, and he didn't see any other reason to stay clean. I found out about his death on Facebook. He was the first overdose in our group. His parents didn't allude to his cause of death, but for us, they didn't have to. We knew.

It was moth season here in Albuquerque. Rivers of moths moved streetlamp to streetlamp once the sun was in her nod. I envied them, having the company of each other, wings grazing wings in play. Somehow, moths always manage to make it into homes by the hundreds. One has to avoid touching their wings or else moths lose their ability to fly. I watched one moth, distanced from the others, dance on a lampshade. I thought of Ryan and how delicate navigating sobriety can be. I thought about fentanyl and how deadly it is. I considered Ryan's yellow hair and slim build. I imagined his last view of some wall with a thick black crack in it. I thought about the other active addicts that may have rifled through his pockets before he was dragged to some corner and left for dead.

I had no one to hug. There were no hands to hold me as I cried. There was no consoling rub on my back—just a Zoom meeting, squares housing faces for me to stare at. Staying clean became a constant debate between two parts of my brain. I wondered how long it would be before it was my turn to disappoint everyone—the coffin, the kind words, the poems on social media about me, the joy my ex-wife would have in knowing I'm really gone.

*

After some weeks, still in quarantine, I began to feel better. Another morning meditation, another gratitude list, another wide sky hosting the sun. I began wearing new shirts, with one shoulder exposed. My eyeliner thickened, and the world appeared prettier than I'd ever known. I found my thumbs frolicking through new books of poetry; Ilya Kaminsky, Li-Young Lee, Jericho Brown ... I began reading a small essay each day by Ross Gay—learning how to find joy in each day. My reflection became more and more tolerable, perhaps even likable. No, lovable!

I read *A God in the House: Poets Talk About Faith* and came across an excerpt by Li-Young Lee:

> "Sometimes a poem comes out and it's done. Sometimes it takes a long time. I do sense when I'm revising that it's about balance between fate and destiny, and chance."

My fate, my destiny, my chance, I thought. *This is my life. These are our lives! I can do anything I want with this life. I am choosing the life I am living. I am a poem the universe is writing.*

Marissa called me. I hadn't spoken to her since rehab, with the exception of small check-ins. I answer only to hear sobs.

"John?"

"Hey lady!"

"John, Bailey died."

I was nine months sober. I had just started back to work since the quarantine orders relaxed. The restaurant I was serving at was allowed twenty-five percent capacity. On a smoke break outside, my cigarette tasted sour.

"No, Marissa, please, oh God, no, no, no ..."

"I didn't want you to find out on Facebook."

My face cooled where tears trailed. She was so tiny, all of her fate and destiny and chance within her grasp. Fuck this world.

"Thanks, Marissa. I gotta go."

That night, I thought about elephants and how they grieve. I imagined myself wrapping my trunk around a tusk of Bailey's and taking it with me. I wanted to wail and throw objects. I wanted to blame the rehab that released her early when Bailey's insurance wouldn't pay for any more treatment. I wanted to blame drug dealers and Purdue Pharmaceuticals. But, in the end, it was Bailey's choice to use again. I stared at that night sky and resented stars for having the audacity to shine. Then, I forgave Bailey. It took some time, but I understood the feeling of resolve we addicts have—that concrete conclusion that this world deals too many obstacles in a day.

Korbin was there for me, by phone, when Ryan and Bailey were no more. In October, I had ten months clean. Korbin and I decided to have lunch the following week to celebrate. Some days went by, and I hadn't heard from Korbin. He had recently celebrated a year clean. I admired him for getting clean so much earlier. He was engaged to a beautiful young woman who was about to have their baby. I knew how busy he was. I was patient. When weeks had gone by, I grew frustrated. It's one thing to be busy. It's another thing to blow people off.

A second quarantine began in New Mexico. My job closed down and I found myself home alone once more, doing my best to read and write, having already lost two friends, and feeling the emptiness that is the holiday season with no family. By this time, I had started wearing long skirts and even glitter in my eyeshadow. I felt at home in my home for the first time in my life. I was grateful for all the hours I spent in solitude, getting to know the new me and having the time to appreciate my life.

Another week passed when I found the post on Facebook. Korbin's mother posted the announcement that he took his life.

I felt nothing; not the wind or sun, my own breath or sadness. To this moment, I haven't felt a thing. So, here I am, seated at a desk, newly divorced, newly rehabilitated, on antidepressants, three friends gone, and wearing makeup.

Quarantine has afforded me a great epiphany: the difference between isolation and solitude. Isolation is a running away from anything or anyone that asks me to look at myself, while solitude welcomes me to experience introspection. These months inside have enabled me to carve a smaller world for me to consider. That doesn't mean I don't still hurt for Palestinians or George Floyd or Breonna Taylor. It means I'm paying more attention to how I participate in this sometimes volatile, sometimes loving world. I've taken the time to ask whatever God exists to root me where I can bloom. I have rested in the dark and contemplated light. I've watched sunrises and considered survival.

I've cried over loss and smiled about the memories I've shared with loved ones. I've learned that my ego loves no one—not even me. I meditate to remind myself that any singular feeling I'm experiencing affects my body the way my presence on this earth affects the entire planet. I see that my life is only as important as I make it; to myself, to others, and to the life itself.

There will come a day when I can kiss cheeks and hug freely those I care for. Connection, or the lack thereof, has taught me that love exists even when I am not aware or interested in its presence. Paying attention to love—to opportunities where I may express it, to those I know, and those I don't—has been my job all along.

Everyone will die. This truth has grown louder now that I have more years behind me than in front of me. My purpose here is to love as many people as I can before my last breath.

Sometimes, that means distancing myself from others in order to love myself. Other times, it means loving others enough to distance myself from them. And still, there are times when I need to be in closer proximity to others because my own mind is trying to kill me. Don't let me die alone.

Quarantine has shown me that death is nothing to be afraid of. What I *do* fear is dying and those closest to me finding out on social media—meaning, I lost touch, imploded, allowed my spirit to be crushed by all the sadness in the world. There are many worlds on this planet. I need to make conscious decisions about what world I want to dwell in.

Whenever it is that I die, I hope I shared in your world, and I hope your world was in love, full of mouths in colorful sound, leaves that could spring back to branches—a world where death deserves a celebration as opposed to torrential questions. May we all have the time to ponder, to propound whether or not we are honest with ourselves about how we walk this place.

2 0/20 has mostly been used in relation to our eyesight—perfect 20/20 vision being the desired norm. I've been wearing glasses to improve my vision for at least 12 – 15 years, but they don't make corrective lenses that can help navigate the year 2020.

20/20 hindsight with respect to where we are now was fully evident in 2016 to anyone paying attention to the political landscape. But nobody ever thought things could get as bad as they are, what with a worldwide pandemic wreaking economic havoc, major (mental and physical) health issues, dramatic adjustments to our everyday routines, and all of it compounded by a political party that holds no regard for human life. Plus, on top of everything else, an incompetent, narcissistic asshole for a president.

Being in the music/hospitality business for over 40 years has been the basis of pretty much all of my friendships, relationships, livelihood, marriage, family, and way of life. The day-to-day busy work that I have performed over the past couple decades has melted away, pretty much, with days punctuated by random flurries of emails moving shows around, filling out various grant applications in the hopes that we can obtain funding from any government sources that are offering, reading the news and hoping for something that will change everything. It never comes. There are times when you think, *This is it, this will end the long nightmare!* And I'm not even talking about COVID here. Even with the election of a new president, it is never ending.

Anytime I have a conversation with friends—whether via text, phone, or in person—the topic of discussion always turns back to what atrocities have been committed by the Trump administration, abetted by the weak-spined members of the GOP.

A neighbor put up a small "Trump/Pence" sign in their yard prior to the election—I live in a zip code that is heavily democratic in composition. I don't know these neighbors at all, but I decided to send them a respectful letter asking them to reconsider and pointing out all of the failings and utter mismanagement of all aspects of government. I didn't really expect to change their minds, but I did want to point out these things. A few days after I mailed the letter, they put up a "Trump/Pence" flag five times bigger than the sign and also spray painted "Trump" on all sides of their plastic trash bin, which I found amusing and insightful. They have since taken down the sign and flag, but the spray painted "Trump" still adorns their trash bins. The irony is obviously lost on them, but at least they came to terms with the result of the election, it would seem.

The pandemic situation we're in has caused me, my wife, and my friends/musical community to sit back and think about what is important—obviously our health, but more than that, respect and empathy for our fellow human beings. Awareness has been raised on so many levels by the actions of our government and the response to those actions by the citizenry. We miss live music, camaraderie with our fellow friends and citizens, being able to walk around without a mask, being able to hug our friends and loved ones.

Most of my friends are cognizant of the dangers of COVID and follow safe practices in our day-to-day routines. We see those who don't believe or who downplay the situation, and they try to act as if the rules and the disease don't apply to their lives. Irresponsibility has become a way of life in the United States—pushed by the stay-in-power-at-any-cost GOP party. A party on the very wrong side of history, a party hankering to go back to whatever utopia they think existed in the Fifties and Sixties.

I've had many friends lose their businesses during the past eight months, and many more who are struggling to find their way through to the other side, which will not be until next spring if everything goes well. I find myself in a Groundhog Day state of existence—getting up every day to go through the same tasks, broken up only by visits to the two businesses that are still operating, or grocery store trips, or the occasional patio dining scenario.

What started out in March as a version of, say, *28 Days Later*, with deserted streets, sparse crowds at beaches and parks, empty shelves and rationing of essential items at grocery stores, has sadly given way to routines involving masks, hand sanitizer, and maintaining distance between each other. We rejoice in any sort of activity that seems to recall "normal" times—a small gathering of like-minded friends, an opportunity to see a live band streaming from any stage anywhere, heading out to the mountains or desert where you can be free in the wilderness, both physically and mentally.

2020 has been a year of living dangerously, if only in the uncertainty of whether any activity you engage in will result in you catching COVID, possibly being hospitalized, or dying. We think we have it figured out and look to the year 2021 with hope, fear, longing, and desire.

ALLY HENNY

was born and raised in rural America. Although I would like to consider myself to be somewhat "citified" at this point in my life, the truth is that I am still just somebody's country cousin who moved to the Windy City. When the pandemic hit, I thought that my husband, kids, and I were the ones who were in the most immediate danger and that the rest of our extended family—who live in rural Missouri—would be safe from the pandemic. I was wrong.

For the first several months of the pandemic, it seemed like my little hometown had things under control. There had been a few cases, but community spread was minimal. While numbers surged in St. Louis, Kansas City, and Springfield—Missouri's population centers—the virus seemed to be controlled elsewhere. Looking back, I think that this might have given people a false sense of security.

At the beginning of November, I received a group text from my mother-in-law informing my husband, his siblings, and I that my father-in-law had tested positive for COVID-19. He had a fever and a runny nose. I felt sad, angry, and scared.

I was sad because we had just reached 200,000 COVID deaths and I didn't want my father-in-law to be one of them.

I was angry because I had long suspected that people weren't taking COVID precautions seriously, which meant that his diagnosis was likely a harbinger of a potential surge.

I felt scared because a surge would mean that the small Black community in my hometown would be at a greater risk and that the rest of my family, including my mom, was in danger.

Something that one must understand about small towns in America is that they are insulated from a lot of the things that we hear and read about on the news. Community violence, mass shootings, protests, bombings, and even global pandemics seem like they are taking place in another world. For a lot of small-town folks, their town is the center of the world, and if they don't encounter certain issues firsthand, it is almost as if they don't exist. A lot of outsiders wrongly call people who think this way "low-information," which simply isn't true.

It's not that people in rural America are "low-information." This is a condescending view that people in positions of privilege and power say about everyone else. It's not rooted in reality. The truth is that rural America often relies on alternative sources because they frequently have to interpret and contextualize information that comes from the mainstream. Information that is geared toward the urban and suburban contexts doesn't always apply to or include rural folks.

For example, I was in high school (if not college) before the news stations in Kansas City started putting my little town on the weather map. That seems trivial, but that little piece of information can mean the difference between knowing whether a little or a lot of rain is coming, getting caught in an ice storm, or being in a tornado.

We expect people to trust and heed information from sources that barely acknowledge certain folks' existence, and then we act surprised when these same people don't see the value in the information that they're given. I don't say this to justify the widespread rejection of masks by certain parts of the populace, but to offer something besides the caricature of red-hat-wearing conspiracy theorists who reject the existence of the virus.

The caricature has some grounding in reality, but there are a lot of folks out there who are being affected by the virus who want nothing to do with the caricature. Additionally, the caricature of Trump-supporting COVID deniers all but erases the Black people who also inhabit rural communities. Black people live in rural America, and they are being affected by the virus.

There's a saying that goes, "When white America gets a cold, Black America gets pneumonia." If the white inhabitants of rural America get cold-like symptoms, many of their Black neighbors will get COVID pneumonia. Literally. Over the past month, several of my close relatives have tested positive for the virus. As I write this, two of them are receiving care in Kansas City. I know of two more of our Black family friends who are at the same hospital.

NPR recently did a story on how the hospitals in Kansas City are seeing an influx of patients from rural counties. Beds are filling up quickly, and the hospitals are worried that there may not be enough beds for everyone when Kansas City's COVID numbers start to surge again. I hope that this doesn't happen, but I can't help but wonder who will be turned away if it does. I can't help but think of the role that systemic racism will play in these decisions.

As COVID-19 tears through rural America, it would be all too easy for us to think that it is only affecting conspiracy-believing anti-maskers. It's not. It is affecting people who are trying to keep themselves and others safe. It is affecting people who think that they are insulated from "big city" problems. It's affecting Black, Brown, and Indigenous folks who are already trying to survive the racism that runs rampant in these towns. Don't forget about rural America, but most of all, don't forget about the racial minorities who live there.

ZAJI COX

Underneath the harsh grocery store lights, the rush of the checkout line provided just enough overwhelm of bodies and carts and voices for my seven-year-old self to only stand and observe. Whenever I stood there with my mom, I simply waited, listening to crinkling bags, the way people's voices moved up and down in small talk, children like me speaking and moving with ease. Standing at the line was an opportunity to take in and receive information. I was able to analyze human behavior.

Since I was very young, I have felt unmeshed with society. Once I got older, I knew this was not unique to me, but as a child I often wondered at the way people would act. I felt like I was on the outside staring in—and being a kid with Asperger's likely played a large part of it. But I didn't mind; I was an observer and have been my whole life. It was a part of my identity that felt natural. The actions of others fascinated me, and while I communicated well as a high-functioning autistic, I felt more understood by our two black cats than anyone else.

As I grew, I was able to study and mimic others, finding my groove in friend groups as a teen, and then more with the general public as an adult. Social media for the most part baffled me and continues to do so, but I was starting to feel good about my relationship with society. This was well through 2019.

Then, 2020 came. Suddenly, I am seven again in an overwhelming world of lights-noise-people, in a world of too-fast change, only able to watch and wonder at the tendencies of others as we are faced with the unfamiliar.

At an early age, I became a master. Observation was soon less of a conscious choice and more a part of my being. I felt like a spectator to the rest of the world, someone watching from afar. With the exception of close family, I looked up at most adults with confusion: Why were they trying so hard to be the same as each other? And what was more, why did they often mistake their tendencies for originality?

Fast-forward to adulthood, where the same questions have begun to arise once again as I watch the screens of my computer and phone flood with hashtags. Themes like *togetherness* and *self-care* start trending, friends post about how much they aren't going outside, Stay Home memes circulate in an effort to feel connected. It all moves too quickly for me, and I feel on the edge once again as an observer. I feel tired. It is all so necessary, so positive—and yet, in this time when togetherness is of utmost importance, it's reminding me of how separate I feel. I'm doing my part—washing my hands has always been important, but suddenly it's more popular than ever before—but I choose not to post about it.

And so, I start to feel annoyed. Maybe a little disdainful. Just when I'd begun to feel more like a part of the social wave, I feel separate once more, watching the wave from afar. How the current shifts. Guessing where it will go next.

Then, there are masks. Being autistic, I've had to work extra hard to understand what otherwise comes naturally to others when it comes to nonverbal signals, but now with half of people's faces hidden, we have to rely more on the nonverbal than ever before. What better way to make me work on my communication skills than government-required face coverings?

In middle school, I realized that to change for the majority I would have to change myself. A few months into classes, I began to feel apart from my own generation; I heard other kids laughing at cruel jokes and awkwardly swearing because they heard it somewhere and thought it was cool. I could see, too, that they wanted others to think it was original. Perhaps they themselves thought it was. I saw what made other kids liked and where their sense of belonging came from. But I soon found myself laughing at the mean jokes, too. I started changing myself to fit in, suppressing the parts of myself that made me unique.

Social norms, trends, rules—things moved quickly, almost too quickly for me to keep up. And it all felt superficial. I was too hyper-aware to not notice the ways in which I was changing, the miniscule things I was doing to myself. So, I left to start homeschooling.

Nowadays, I see swells and falls of hashtags and trends, *stay together* intermixing with *keep your distance*. Fearmongering, information that contradicts itself, friends shunning and condemning friends based on the ability to follow rules that change weekly and often daily. I soon made it a point to ask, "What is your source for that information?"

It's something like a film plot—a globe falling under a single threat. It crept in from the outside and soon forced us apart within months, offering an edge-of-your-seat surreality from which you disconnect to process fully. I've been watching the nation—the world—use social media both to respond and connect; and being someone who was the last of their high school friends to get a Facebook page, I felt disconnected. And not in the way of social distance.

To be honest, it's likely just me getting tired of social media. It's a confusing experience. I've taken breaks and stayed off my phone for lengths of time, but there is no better way to promote myself and my art right now. Other than connecting with close friends and family, that is why I use it.

And, to be honest, pockets of positivity—activism through art, new ways of connecting long-distance—brighten the experience. Not to mention virtual opportunities for artists.

The new lights-noise-people of the modern world for me might be the endless scrolls of Facebook and Instagram, but I am learning to adjust. It makes the weirdness of feeling unmeshed with society, and the experience of 2020, a little more manageable.

"**D**o you feel like you made it?" A confidant asked. "Sometimes," I said. "Sometimes I feel like I made it." A notion is to think it means, "success." To me, it means, *I survived*. The feeling of success is fleeting, while the need to survive is eternal. A way forward before my time, I'm sure, but now is a generational curse that refuses to be undone.

According to my goal-oriented Excel spreadsheet, for the last two and a half years, I applied to 179 jobs (67 of them were part- and full-time teaching jobs) before landing a tenure track English teaching position at a community college. I should have celebrated this huge feat accomplished without a Ph.D. I should have cried happy tears that I outperformed hundreds of other applicants. Instead, I barely shared it with loved ones. Then, two months later, I nonchalantly made an update on my LinkedIn profile. Why? While the world faces a global pandemic, I feel unauthorized to have a solid year.

Although 2020 has been my breakout year, COVID-19 has amplified uncertainty on too many fronts, such as job security, healthcare, and being Black in America. All three hit home for me. Months prior, I juggled adjunct teaching, creative workshops, and hustling poetry books. Was, is, adjunct teaching secure? Not really. Between teaching at three different colleges, I could guestimate teaching a course at one, maybe two of them, which meant my income was a living, breathing variable.

Shockingly, I made just enough, as long as an emergency never happened. Guess what? Several did. Navigating from my Westchester, NY apartment to a Montclair, NJ classroom without a car is a three-hour-each-way nightmare. It was overcome with an eventual car purchase, but was replaced with an unbearable toothache at the beginning of COVID-19. And New York was placed on PAUSE; Governor Cuomo issued an executive order that closed 100% of non-essential businesses statewide. It was mission impossible to get detailed tooth work done, regardless that I was also underinsured. Maybe if the pain hadn't randomly stopped, I would have found an endodontist (or made myself) to immediately pull it out.

Did I mention a book tour that was planned for six months was also COVID-19 canceled?

Before *The Blues Cry For A Revolution*, my poetry collection that speaks to the systemic oppression of Black people in the U.S., was published in January 2020, I held a strong belief that my country was ripe for actionable steps that could change Black lives for the better. What I didn't know was that it would take a COVID-19 worldwide shutdown and the all too familiar and inexcusable Black deaths of George Floyd and Breonna Taylor to build traction against the many systems of oppression prevalent in all areas of Black life. Still, in many instances, generational hardships were placated with symbolic gestures, like firing Aunt Jemima. A true difference would be to build on the work of countless Black scholars and activists and everyday working-class people to change lives for generations to come.

Somewhere between writing about Black life and living it, my survival instincts are triggered. I am a storyteller who finds it difficult to understand that a survival story is one out of many. Instead, survival is on constant replay. Case in point: Cooking salmon and shrimp for the same dinner is a decision I won't make. Maybe because, growing up, Mom was only able to cook lavishly on holidays or special occasions. It ain't about the price, both are purchased and in the freezer. It is survival masquerading as fear—things will go wrong without a way to ease them. It is not being able to see myself thriving from a place of privilege or a place of progression, during and after COVID-19, with a straight face.

During COVID-19 where online classes are the new normal, I find myself staring at impressionable faces through Zoom. Between brief moments of silence and writing, I think about how I have an opportunity to pour into 60 – 80+ scholars a semester, like the countless people who've poured into me. Within the parameters of Intro to English 101, I aim to create a curriculum and course experience that is both challenging and rewarding. The goal is hefty to teach the whole person not just what's needed for class but to thrive in the world.

Thriving in my world is rediscovering biking, which I did as a kid with my Brooklyn family. The breeze against my face peddling up and down Westchester has created a sense of normalcy against the backdrop of insurmountable COVID-19 changes. It is socially distant yet familiar enough to connect with old friends and make new ones. When I am biking, I am a person who is thriving in spite of COVID-19.

I just didn't know there was a learning curve to thriving. Despite that, I don't have to live as if survival is a mode or mood. After, *I survived*, I must continue anew. I must tell myself a thriving story that reimagines models of possibilities that can become transformative sparks for myself and scholars and others. Even if shifting my mindset to normalize thriving while Black, like teaching, like writing, like biking uphill, is a herculean task.

When I was a kid, my favorite game was pretending I lived alone. I constructed a one-bedroom apartment in my imagination, a bubble where everything was clean and new and only mine. In my fantasies, I awoke every morning on a queen-sized bed, and I spent most of my time reading and drinking tea. In reality, I shared a room with my siblings, and I slept on a mattress that pulled out from under a bunk bed. Our room was always messy, and never quiet. While I washed piles of dishes, I plotted my escape. I'd imagine moving out of my parents' house once I turned eighteen, away from their chaos, and I'd never move back.

My parents said my younger siblings and I were the reason they migrated to the United States from Argentina. Maybe that's part of the reason I spent much of my life thinking that "up," "forward," and "away" were the only directions I should aspire to move towards. I idealized the concept of advancement. I watched my parents manage two jobs, four kids, and multiple side hustles. I accepted that I had to work constantly to move towards the front of the line. I had to be the first. I had to do the most. I had to be the best. I had to make their sacrifice worth it.

Before the shelter-in-place order was announced, I was living in the Bay Area with my husband. I worked several jobs while I attended grad school. Most days, we sat at our separate desks working from early morning until late at night and, at the end of the day, we still beat ourselves up for not doing enough. Other times, on slow-brewing Sunday mornings, I felt like I was living my childhood fantasy. We awoke on a huge blue bed. We read novels in our matching-striped hammocks. We cooked late breakfasts. We ate our meals on a checkered tablecloth, and we were happy.

A few weeks following COVID, I received a call from my dad. After my parents' divorce, my mother stayed close to LA, and my father bought a fixer-upper in a small rural community on the edges of the county. The family catering business made enough money to pay for the mortgage, but his income began to suffer when large gatherings stopped with the pandemic. My father was doing seasonal farm work and handyman jobs around town. He told me he was working five, sometimes six days a week, but he still wasn't making enough money picking grapes, digging holes, and building fences. Then he paused for a moment, and he asked me if my husband and I could move in with him.

I panicked. My immediate response was a definite no.

Weeks later, I still ruminated on the idea. Work wasn't the most stable, and Bay Area rent wasn't getting cheaper. If I moved back to LA, I could help my dad and save some money. It made financial sense. But I was scared to say yes.

I imagined hordes of faceless people mocking me, talking behind my back, calling me a loser. *After all that hard work, after all the degrees*, they'd say, *and she still had to move back*. The moment where I was publicly humiliated by a horde of judgmental over-achievers never came. In fact, many adults of my generation were battling with the same issue. According to the Pew Research Center, before 2020, the highest recorded number of adults living with their parents in the United States was in 1940, after the Great Depression.

I remember what I learned about the Great Depression in high school, the pictures of mothers disfigured by worry, fleeing from the dust bowl with malnourished children at their hips. We were taught their move was vindicated by the sizeable measure of their suffering. I compared it to my life, and my move seemed hardly justifiable. I am not out of work. I am not hungry. I am not homeless. The kid inside me still remembered the sitcom jokes about adults who lived with their parents. They were lazy, dependent blobs that complained about what was for dinner. They were the talentless and the reckless, the ones that failed to see they were the butt of the joke.

I had bought into the idea that "moving forward" is synonymous with "moving away" when I was a child. I thought the only justification for moving back with your parents was a life-threatening event. As an adult, I understood life was a bit more complicated than that, but I never bothered to check back in with myself. Only after I began considering moving back, I began to reject the idea that moving back was synonymous with moving backwards.

I live in my father's house now, with my husband and two of my siblings. My succulents died a couple weeks after I moved in, but I decided to plant some tomatoes instead. I purchased a pair of heavy-duty work boots that cover my ankles to protect me from rattlesnake bites. My lips cracked when the first Santa Ana winds came, and I make time to ride my bike at least three times a week. We have three goats and twenty chickens, and juniper trees with seeds that ripen and litter the ground in October.

Sometimes we have heated arguments over dinner, where I point out my father's sexism or call out my brother on his anger issues, and we go to bed without saying good night. Other times, my dad tells my husband some of my favorite childhood stories, and I hear some new ones I didn't know about. My husband and I chose to put part of our work on hold. He learned how to use the sewing machine and fix his own pants, and I learned how to change the tubes on my bike. We are closer to my in-laws, and my husband has time to walk them through their retirement paperwork. I try to help my dad adjust his business plan to a post-pandemic world.

I live with my dad, but I've learned that maintaining my adultness is less about proving I'm successful and more about letting go of my childhood fantasies. As a kid, I wanted to live in my own bubble. But if there's anything I've learned this year, it's that we are all infinitely and inescapably interconnected. I've learned to slow down. I learned to take self-care more seriously. I've learned to listen more and react less. I've learned to recognize feelings of unproductiveness, which is the first step in trying to let them go. Perhaps the most important thing I learned this year is that I need to detach my self-worth from my productivity. Rest and recovery are not passive. Stillness and introspection take work.

For me, 2020 is a time to reflect every time I take a step forward, and to start normalizing taking a step back.

DECEMBER 2020

DECEMBER 5 – Nationwide COVID-19 cases surpass 15 million, with about one out of every 22 Americans having tested positive since the pandemic began.

DECEMBER 11 – Nationwide COVID-19 cases surpass 16 million; a new single-day record of 280,567 coronavirus cases; and a new single-day record of 3,309 deaths are reported.

DECEMBER 14 – Nationwide COVID-19 cases surpass 17 million.

DECEMBER 15 – President-Elect Joe Biden nominates Pete Buttigieg to be Secretary of Transportation, becoming the first openly gay person appointed to a cabinet-level position, if confirmed.

DECEMBER 17 – President-Elect Joe Biden nominates Deb Haaland for Secretary of the Interior, becoming the first Native American appointed to a cabinet-level position, if confirmed.

DECEMBER 19 – Trump tweets: "Big protest in D.C. on January 6th. Be there, will be wild!"

DECEMBER 19 – Nationwide COVID-19 cases surpass 18 million.

DECEMBER 22 – Trump on coronavirus: "Distribution of both vaccines is going very smoothly. Amazing how many people are being vaccinated, record numbers. Our Country, and indeed the World, will soon see the great miracle of what the Trump Administration has accomplished. They said it couldn't be done!!!"

DECEMBER 23 – Nationwide COVID-19 cases surpass 19 million.

DECEMBER 27 – Trump tweets: "See you in Washington, DC, on January 6th. Don't miss it. Information to follow."

DECEMBER 29 – First US case of new COVID-19 variant found in Colorado.

DECEMBER 29 – Nationwide COVID-19 cases surpass 20 million.

DECEMBER 30 – Trump tweets: "JANUARY SIXTH, SEE YOU IN DC!"

DECEMBER 31 – CDC says that 2,800,000 people have received initial dose of vaccine.

360,766 DEATHS | 20,551,180 INFECTED

TWO THOUSAND TWENTY & THE AGE OF CONSEQUENCE

CHRIS VALLE

I was born in 1970, so I'm used to measuring the chapters of my life in nice, round numbers. I'm not unique in my tendency to arbitrarily group a series of significant events, but as decades go, it's a digestible way to look at things, especially the life of a young country. Without indulging in retrospective, let me just say that the shelves of volumes representing the years between my first and my 50th year will likely get a branding treatment such as "Antebellum" or "Reformation." I would like to propose that we call the last 50 years "Pre-Consequential America." We did what we wanted: Sex, Drugs, Rock & Roll, Death & Taxes, War, Famine ... and the other one ... ah, yes ... Plague.

2020 is the mirror reflecting American society back at itself with staggering and sobering clarity. This is our formal entry into "The Age of Consequence." Every political, social, ecological, cultural, or economic flaw in our society has been thrust back upon us all at once, with a generous helping of bad luck slathered on top. We played ourselves; we laid so many mines and rigged so many booby traps that we ran out of safe places to stand. COVID nudged us just enough to stumble, and then everything just started blowing up.

In no particular order:

We have the legacy of wars on multiple fronts (Afghanistan, Iraq, Syria) that have lasted a generation. By the winter of 2020-21 we will have US servicemembers fighting and dying in a war older than they are.

We are in the grip of a global pandemic that has killed enough Americans to qualify as our third deadliest conflict, if the enemy were human.

We are experiencing sustained and widespread protests against the legacy of American anti-Black racism, the depth and breadth of which can only be referred to glancingly in this format as a *core value of our culture*, preceding the existence of the country itself by more than 150 years, but still being pursued today in the form of mass incarceration, disenfranchisement, undereducation, income and wealth and healthcare disparity, not to mention the summary execution and lynching of Black people by police officers and domestic terrorists.

The status of women, even as women of all ages and backgrounds take their rightful places in leadership roles, is under attack by regressive politics, led most ironically in this country by a judicial appointment of tragically poetic composition. In this year of the 100th anniversary of women's suffrage, it looks like a small number of zealots still have the power to undo generations of progress with the backing of a disturbingly large number of voters.

The impact of climate change and exaggerated weather has begun to flood coastal cities, burn temperate areas, thaw cooler ones, and is a topic of such density that I can only suggest that you seek more thorough descriptions and analyses elsewhere. Briefly? It's bad, and we all know it.

But wait, there's more.

The state of our political institutions, with all the flaws endemic to human administration, is now a Civil Cold War. At every possible juncture, the rule of law is being undermined and disregarded at the highest levels of government. The social and political progress of the last (insert value) years has been met with a backlash that I have dubbed "The Death Rattle of White Patriarchy," a violent and politically extreme movement to undo gains made in voting rights, gender equality, racial justice, economic fairness, LGBTQIA+ representation, land rights of indigenous people, immigration policy, and even staggeringly, public health policy intended to contain and treat the outbreak of the novel coronavirus. Entrenched, hyper-partisan factions have made our government a Zero-Sum scenario and have done the greatest actual harm to citizens since the war between The States. This is a Civil Cold War.

Our economic landscape features staggering wealth held by the tiniest fraction of oligarchs and technocrats, while billions of people worldwide live on pocket change. America, while enjoying relative prosperity for its poorest people, continues to consume and inspire consumption in a manner that makes the term "end-state capitalism" almost flattery, as if this was an actual economic scheme as opposed to a continental smash-n-grab. We're stuck with the ugly bastard of hereditary wealth and a free-market bloodbath.

We are in a perfect storm made of perfect storms. Freddy vs Jason vs Darth Vader vs Agent Smith vs Voldemort vs Sauron vs Thanos vs, well, Donald John Trump. Our murder hornets have come home to roost.

I don't have the stamina, expertise, or background research to delve into any of these massive crises at any responsible length. Let's call them dancefloor shout-outs. ("White supremacy inna house! I see you, Coronavirus! Miami's under water, whaat!" (air horn))

The story of 2020 is the simultaneous onslaught of a comprehensive array of America's worst problems, any one of which could be the life's work of any number of historians. I see your 1776, 1865, 1929, 1941, 1963, 1968, and raise you 2020. This year, even without the benefit of hindsight, is a veritable testbed of the flaws of modern American government, business, and society.

I'm not here to offer solutions ... except, perhaps, "Everyone get right with the idea of doing things differently, because whether you get right or not, we're doing things differently." You're going to be part of the solution, or you will most definitely be the problem. Meaning: imagine giving up your car, changing careers, risking physical violence to protest, putting unreasonable amounts of time and energy into endeavors with no guarantee of success or even progress. Challenge what you believe, because everyone else will be challenging what you believe. It's time for another Greatest Generation. This one will have to be greater still, because we can't nuke our way out of this one. There's no 1950s-style golden era coming on the heels of Afghanistan or COVID. The kids are going to have to be world-builders.

It's been a heartbreaking year as well, obviously because we lost hundreds of thousands of lives to COVID-19, scores of beloved public figures, but on a more personal level for me, because I lost the all-important *benefit of the doubt*. I have to remind myself and accept that the average person is capable of some properly horrific shit, and all you have to do is *give them permission*. Once desperation fuses with disrespect and disregard, you see a critical mass that releases a wide-spectrum destructive attitude normally reserved for "shithole countries," but now being directly self-inflicted in every corner of the nation. Defiantly. Militantly. Like Thích Quảng Đức back in Saigon in 1963 ... except it's idiots & assholes, doing it for the worst reasons, and also burning you up as well.

I'm a flexible cynic, though. I believe in people, but I believe that many of us are just beastly, with none of the redeeming features of actual beasts. Our ability to stand aside and abet brutality is harder to square than brutality itself, and I am guilty of taking little hits of dilute American Exceptionalism to take the edge off, allowing me to think that, within our young, ambitious liberal democracy, we somehow were better at this civilization thing.

I have to remind myself that America was the Teenage Millionaire of the modern world. Our single blew up and we made bank. "Young, scrappy, and hungry" has a lot of sex appeal, and the world forgives a champion ... a champion with a gun, more so. We made a lot of mistakes that we didn't have the wisdom, patience, or moral fiber to examine, especially considering the premise on which the country was founded. Can we be anything but surprised this hasn't blown back sooner? No one else had the leverage to fully prosecute us. Too many wanted a piece of our action or were simply willing to afford us certain liberties in exchange for keeping worse people in check. It was easier to be Germany or Japan if Russia and China were preoccupied with America, and they could get on with building more perfect unions than ours while we shoved one another. Now, we're approaching middle age, and that Bad Boy behavior isn't cute anymore. Your first TV in the hotel pool is a hilarious anecdote. Your ninth is a felony. When Nazi Germany decides your racism is "extra" you should probably check yourself. Three generations later, any remnants of that policy is properly atrocious. The spouse of our ideals crossed paths with the side piece of our baser reality in the Costco parking lot, and they are now furiously clawing at each other on the hot pavement.

I waited until after Election Day 2020 to finish this. Then I waited more. I guessed correctly that the process and outcome of this election/transition would color my assessment of this absolute Tarantino Looney Tune of a year. I watched us squabble, I watched more violence and nonsense, I watched more people die. I watched politicians basically mocking our problems and keeping their jobs. I saw hundreds of millions of people sweat bullets and white-knuckle their way through a year that would, in a better society, be a referendum on basic human values. For us, it was the slap across the face that may at least provoke moments of national introspection.

2020 marks the end of our innocence ... again. We had no right to that delusional state, which was really only our insistent, urgent denial of our trail of tears from the 17th to 21st centuries, but we finally rubbed all the glossy paint off of the façade, and now we are propping up the shaking falsework that we call America. We have barely affirmed our functionality as a nation-state by holding a successful general election—something that developing countries use as "baby steps."

2021 seems poised to be the social and political barroom brawl that 2020 ignited. There's so much in flux, and a sense of focus and commitment to progress within this chaos. I'm hopeful that 2020 did its job and marks the beginning of a new era in the US.

I am my mother's only child.

Diabetes has turned her ankles into fleshy tree trunks, no tapering calves, the skin between the toes startlingly red, toenails the color of toasted milk and thick as bark. She used to make Laban, bring the milk to a boil until it stuck to the pot's edge. She'd skim the caramel-colored frill with a spoon, feed it to me, claiming it would make me strong. I preferred it to the blinding-white Laban. Even in the sticky summer heat, her feet are cold, and when I kneel to pull on her hospital socks, saved from numerous visits to the ER, my fingers leave impressions on her skin.

My father left on their 25th wedding anniversary. It seemed especially cruel then, still does. Even before he disappeared, I felt compelled to fill a void in my mother I couldn't understand or identify and, after all this time, I find myself unable to resolve conflicting feelings. Sometimes, when I'm pushing urine-soaked bedsheets in the wash, the smell gagging me through my mask, I wonder if I am being punished. It's my fault, after all, that she's soaked the bed. "You didn't put the mattress pad under me," she says, repeating it four times, until I walk away. I feel guilty for resenting her. She's ashamed. How do I honor the way her body has betrayed her? I want to excise my resentment, slice it clean out.

"When will they have a vaccine?" she asks, as I pick up a murder of spent tissues on the couch and strewn around her feet. The indented couch cushion, where she spends most of her day napping, reading, watching TV, and the adjoining cushion have become her office. There are stacks of bank statements, receipts, Medicare and Social Security statements, a bamboo back scratcher, tissue boxes, tongs employed to pick up nail file / pen / glasses / remote / stamps / stationary / pen, notes we write to communicate because she is profoundly deaf and refuses to wear hearing aids. "I read lips," she claims. *But my mask*, I want to say.

She lives with us and we do what we can to protect her. At 99, she's become my child. I must protect her because the world will not. I buy diapers and pads and prescriptions and Smucker's low-sugar strawberry jam and Brownberry bread and Nabisco Toasteds (onion-flavored) and Kraft sharp cheddar (it must be sharp) and strawberries without green tops and Butterfingers (don't tell) and cotton balls and Tucks and Folgers coffee. "Did you use the coupons I gave you?" she asks.

Her nurse, who visits every Monday at 11:30, pesters her about her weight. "She has worried about her weight her entire life," I say. "Let her be." What I want to say, *Leave her alone about it already*.

Color. Wash and set. Every two months until the pandemic. Now, I help her into the shower, pull the washcloth over her. The smell of Dial soap fills the humid space. I wash her silver hair but the hair at the nape won't cooperate. It's a Brillo pad of hair. *When did this happen? How could this be?* The water refuses to soak it. Drying her off, getting her into a chair, I cut it as best I can then dye it with drugstore color. Despite my best efforts, her hair turns pink. She moves the mirror back and forth, tilts her head. "I like it," she says, and I think she means it. "Thank you, Honey," she says. Every time I leave, she says: "I love you, Honey. Give the girls a hug."

I do a DNA test and, years later, get an email claiming my mother is the aunt of a woman I've never met. My mother is the only living and youngest of eight children. I have a large and loving Lebanese family. We know each other, grew up together. I ask, "Did Uncle Tommy have a child?" He was a bachelor. It would make sense. "No," she says resolutely. She pauses and I wonder, fleetingly, hopefully, *Could it be my sister?* "No, not Tommy's," she repeats. Pause. She shakes her head. "I've never told anyone this. All these years. I never told anyone.

Tommy and I drove M to a house in Detroit. She was pregnant. Before she was married. I remember crying the whole way home. It was a different time then."

We find out later, after we've been in contact with her newly found niece, that M named her two daughters, the ones born in wedlock and after the baby she gave up for adoption, the same names as the baby's two older sisters. *It was a clue*, I think. *Dear M left a clue.* I find out, too, that when this baby had a serious operation, according to the two older sisters, an "exotic-looking" woman waited with them in the family lounge. *Was it M? Did M know the adoptive parents of her child?*

She loved this baby, wholly and desperately, but gave her up. My new cousin writes my mother, her aunt, every week. My mother yearns to meet her, but during a pandemic it's too dangerous.

My father, who left but came back into my life when he became ill, who I did not care for physically like I do my mother, recovered in a nursing home after hip surgery. "It's a rule," they said. "Rehab facility," they called it. It smelled of shit and urine. One day, during a visit, we went into the lounge. He read the *Flint Journal* while I tried to think of safe topics to discuss, something besides asking, *Why did you ignore me for two decades?* A little woman, her skin the color of ash, eyes rheumy, sits next to me holding a wad of blankets. My father looks over the newspaper, shakes it, resumes reading. "I can't find my baby," she says, her voice desperate. "Your baby?" "Yes. I can't find it. It was just here." "Where?" "Here," she says, pointing to the blankets. My father shakes his head, warning me off, but I disregard him. I unravel the flannel bundle, a multi-layered cocoon. When I pull away the last layer, revealing the bundle's middle, I find a bloody mucus plug (to this day I can't identify, exactly, what it was). I flinch, grazing the little woman's nose with my hand. She wails like a wounded animal.

I will do anything to keep my mother out of a nursing home.

She's on the floor, on her back, unable to move. It's March 2020 and the pandemic has hobbled Chicago, the world. She'd called but I had been on the phone, declined the call, didn't listen to the message. When I get there, 30 minutes later, I curse myself for not answering. I help her sit, get her up, ask if she's in pain. "The hip," I ask, "does your hip hurt?" We're both trembling. There will be no hospital visit, no nurse. Elderly people are dying and there's a general sense of helplessness and confusion about why and how. I call her doctor and he says to "sit tight, don't let anyone in the house, check for bruising." For the next three months, I dress her, bathe her, make her meals, help her in and out of the bathroom, get her in bed, tuck her in, turn off the lights.

Years ago, a physical therapist came to the house to evaluate her. She's so small, barely five feet, the spinal stenosis compressing her year by year. He put his arms around her roughly, as if hoisting a bag of dirt, turned her around with his hands against her breasts. "What are you doing?" I asked, livid. "Why are you treating her like that?" He looked at me as if no one had ever said that to him before.

She's made mujadara but she didn't use enough onions, the bulgur is hard, and the lentils barely cooked. "It's good," I say, lying. "Your dad used to like this," she says. We rarely speak of my father. "Do you pray for him?" I hadn't been, praying for him, and the realization surprises me. "You should pray for him," she says.

I do.

She runs out of adult diapers and I'm forced to go to Walgreens. Before I leave, she pushes coupons into my palm. As I'm checking out, a young man stands behind me. Twenties. Buying White Claw. The cashier is having trouble with the multiple coupons I've supplied, the ones my mother insisted would work. They're expired, of course, I should have checked, and the cashier, bless her heart, is now looking at the weekly flyer. "I know there's a coupon here somewhere," she says. The young man sighs, shifts from foot to foot. I want to slap him. After an interminable time, I say, "Never mind, it's okay." "You sure?" the cashier asks, eyeing me. "Yeah," I say, as the line extends to the photo department. "These diapers are expensive, just trying to save you a little money." She seems hurt.

I return to my mother, produce the receipt like a child. My mother gets out her mini flashlight, reads the receipt. "Didn't use the coupons," she says.

After my father is kicked out of assisted living for dementia-related antics including but not limited to walking into a freezing night barefoot, in his pajamas, and calling one of the men who captured him a "fat fuck," he asks if he can live with me. "Mom lives with us," I say, "so, you can't." "I've forgotten why I left her," he says. "Well, she hasn't," I say.

The first time he left, I returned from my summer job to find her in our evening-shadowed family room, curled up on the couch. "He left," she said. "Where'd he go?" I asked stupidly. "He left me." He would return. Then leave. Return. Leave. Who knows how many times. Finally, he left for good. It must have been during this time that I glimpsed the future. It must have been during this time that I began holding my mother together. She's held me together too, of course, more than I can quantify. The lines blur. I acknowledge my limitations, know it's impossible to soothe the desperately maintained aching parts, raw with hurt, hidden from view.

LINDA RAND

When self-quarantine first began in March, I slept A LOT. It felt like a necessity, and even my toddler was very sleepy. We would have a five-hour nap, then be up for a few hours, and then go right back to bed again, snuggled up with each other, her little compact body warm, the soft puffs of breath from her tiny round nostrils infinitely comforting.

I made a lot of immune boosters, spicy fire cider, and for the toddler it was cut with elderberry juice and honey. I took echinacea tincture and ate raw garlic so hot and potent I felt that I injured myself. I drank celery juice, bee pollen, coconut water, coffee, green tea. I couldn't really eat. I couldn't really read books. I couldn't really watch anything, plus the characters kept breathing all over each other and didn't keep six feet away.

My glands were swollen. I was afraid of what could happen to Frida if I fell ill, my ex/her father on vacation in Hawaii, her grandparents at risk in California, unable to fly. I thought of Human Services taking her away, as everyone was sequestered in their own homes. I *couldn't* get sick. I read about a nurse who died and, when they found her, her young child was curled up nearby. My worst fears had happened to someone else. So devastating.

I'd pick up a book but still could not focus, except when staying up all night finding everything I could about COVID online and watching what was happening in Bergamo, Italy. I started cooking and freezing things, talking with people on the phone. I'd eat apple skins, giving the flesh to the kids; I ate leftover scraps, felt good about how long the food would last. I'd open the pantry and stare. I'd imagine how many days it would last for the kids, and in what combinations. Then, I'd think of what the next perishable item would be and how we'd eat that first.

By the third week, my daughter's dad was back in town and wanted to see her. I, of course, said a two-week quarantine was mandatory before discussing visitation; but just knowing I wasn't the only adult relieved some psychological stress. I was beginning to read again! I thought about things other than COVID occasionally.

We started gardening and planted sugar snaps and kitchen scraps that sprouted, like purple cabbage, onion, carrots, and celery. I cut back a lot of blackberry canes, raked decomposing leaves unearthing a dark, lush soil that smelled so good it made my mouth water, reminded me of the forest. My daughter happily collected white camellia petals, saying they were onions. She lined them up in the raised bed, sprinkled dirt on each one, and then watered them.

I started fantasizing about visiting a secret wild place away from any town, where there would be no people, a roaring river. Maybe when the toddler could see her dad again, I'd reward myself, the first time alone in months. Just the teasing thought was nourishment to me, imagining my naked feet on warm rock. I had to remember to start the car occasionally in the evening. I'd sit inside and it smelled clean and fresh like a rental car and the interior lights would cast their amber hue. The little dinging sound, which might have been mildly annoying before, was cozy and faintly exciting. I'd start the engine and remember that I was a person who used to go places.

At the beginning of the pandemic, I posted a daily diary knowing that at some point I'd lose track of the days as life became more normalized. The last numbered day was 131 back in July, more than four months ago. That was when I was still able to participate in the nightly protests in Portland for BLM, right before it became necessary to start wearing a gas mask because it was so "spicy" with heavy tear gas. I actually looked at different masks online while considering how to continue. But after 1000s of Portlanders from all walks of life began to protest against the Feds and BORTEC, I found myself slipping into soul-saving nature and exploring the possibility of a new relationship with a human I had started hanging out with right before the city shut down.

Finally having access to the forest soothed a burning angst, to find solace in something older than our civilization that made little sense these days and being held in adult human arms helped quell a fiery, crazy-making skin hunger. It was incredible to realize how much touch we took for granted pre-pandemic, casual social touch, hugs, the brush of fingers on a hand, a pat on the shoulder. After months of not interacting with another adult in the flesh, I felt so fortunate to finally be able to rest with another human, legs and arms entwined, as the echoing chants, probably a symptom of mild PTSD, began to slowly dissipate in my head, *"A.C.A.B., ALL COPS ARE BASTARDS, A.C.A.B., ALL COPS ARE BASTARDS," "WHOSE STREETS? OUR STREETS! WHOSE STREETS? OUR STREETS! WHOSE STREETS? OUR STREETS!" "STAY TOGETHER, STAY TIGHT, WE DO THIS EVERY NIGHT! STAY TOGETHER, STAY TIGHT, WE DO THIS EVERY NIGHT!" and "HEY HEY, HO HO, THESE RACIST COPS HAVE GOT TO GO! HEY HEY, HO HO, THESE RACIST COPS HAVE GOT TO GO!"*

Then, the fires came. The skies turned ocher with ash fluttering down of charred forest animals and trees. You could taste past lives in the ash, tiny and delicate like snowflakes, the farm in the forest I found refuge in, on Level Two. Level One is to be on alert. Level Two is a significant risk. Level Three is GO NOW!

Revelation is an apocalyptic book with monsters, seismic events, and horsemen that annihilate one-third of the population. This culminates in the creation of a new and better heaven and earth, as the old one is destroyed. The pandemic in its disruptive nature set the stage for an unveiling. It ruptured our mass hypnosis that allowed us to continue to ignore decades of dire warnings. Only with the abrupt and inexorable worldwide breakdown of our regular patterns could we have the possibility to establish new patterns other than the kyriarchy we live in, with its limitations of existence as either being oppressed or privileged.

In those early days of sequestering, faced with only ourselves, we had the chance to integrate our shadow self, the part we want to vilify in others. We also couldn't help but notice how blue the skies and water had become as pollution dropped, and animals thrived when the humans had to stay inside. 2020 had started out as an apocalyptic year starting with Australia on fire and koala bears being deemed "functionally extinct," a quick phase of murder hornets, and then, of course, COVID with 1.47 million deaths worldwide, as I'm writing this, and with the 268,000 U.S. deaths expected to double by the end of the year. There have been travel bans, the West Coast on fire, threats of our Postal Service being dismantled. The deep divide in our country has been revealed. The lack of equity with care and testing unavailable in lower income neighborhoods. The ageism as COVID has ravaged through nursing homes. The racism as COVID has burned through Native American tribal communities. People worldwide fed up with sanctioned police violence, taking to the streets in protest supporting Black Lives Matter.

To sum up this year has been impossible because it feels like we are still emerging. I've learned that, with every fear I've confronted, there is a moment of rest, then a readying for the next, like labor pains. 2020 is the year of birth. It is an initiation into a new era of continuous change. Many people act as if things will magically be "normal" when this year is over, but I think this year has intimated that it is only the beginning—a preparation for what's to come.

1

As we shelter-in-place, the anthill becomes our cityscape, the only bustle of activity within miles of the house we have grown into never leaving. Two feet tall, tucked into a neighboring manzanita below the slumped whorl of pink flowers that blossomed the first week after rain, a silent industry building the hilltop surrenders no clue to the drama beneath. A universe in what looks like an overturned basket. Dirt, nettles, movement, dried leaves, close to the road but shaded for the queen who waits beneath, full-bellied, newly home from her nuptial flight and anticipating the eggs to follow. Unaware in her ripe fullness of spring, of any earthly reason to leave.

2

A cookout feet away, the domestic tragedy on a hot day of Coke spilled. Ice locks together on the sidewalk, an intimate berg. Beneath the sun, a melt of white light, of luxury, those rare, cool diamonds dissected in the inner murmur of mound gossip, worker gossip. A rumor so unbelievably untrue now true, and so unbelievably cold, sweet as, helpless, we watch a highway of red and black operatives storm the slick puddle of fizz. They float their bodies, euphoric, along the carbon dioxide bubbles until caramel color and corn syrup stop up their gears, heads down, abdomens stuck in what we can imagine from old biology textbooks to be their mouths drawing in the toxic gift. Too many bodies for us to gather on a twig, emigrants we try to move with the emergency order of our fingers to dry ground, past the next wall of pine needles to land like foreigners on the soil of another hill's birth.

3

Their hive mind chooses to congregate, build, construct a new hill in our driveway. Ants are never victims of transverse orientation, but we always find a moth flapping in a spiderweb or drowning in the bedside water glass. Why compare ants to moths, us to any living thing? Me with my shovel trying to scoot a universe over a foot to the left. How will we get the mail in the middle of an anthill, take out the garbage cans, bring in the paper? It is no use, of course, to slide a building, and how is this monument any different? As the mound collapses in on itself it reveals its inner sanctum of secrets, dozens of milky white egg sacs. Disturbed nursery sleepers, shocking in their translucence, almost like spying on a beautiful woman through a sheer blind.

4

I set the shovel against a tiny yellow rose bush, for the first time in decades budless, and blame, somehow, the anthill for the bush's demise. I can at the very least rescue these eggs from the concrete, wet from the lawn sprinkler, but my hands are too big, clumsy, all thumbs. They are nothing like the cocoons from the caterpillars that covered the house one summer, grey green spun ovals. Felted wool we dared to finger after the caterpillars took to the sky, a tear in their cloth that told us the discarded husks belonged to no one. Our spell to touch was brief, young girls more interested in dialing and hanging up on boys, but we spent enough time sticking our fingers in spaces hollowed out by the progress of bodies becoming better versions of themselves.

5

The day after I try to hose away the larvae I thought had perished at the end of our driveway, the carnage like a set of teeth punched from their mouth in a fight, I see a flurry of movement. Thatcher ants, I look up online, carrying the burden to restock their nursery until every last egg finds a soft place to rest away from the one who wields the shovel. The one who, months before the massacre, first tried displacing the burgeoning mound with the leaf blower, unused because we live in an area without many leaves. I had only spied a few black wriggles, some holes in the dirt close to where we walk, drive, weekly set out the recycle can, so I blew the dirt back under the apple tree in hopes they would take a hint. How trespassers will always be punished, though I knew they could never understand the concept of boundary lines, walls. My own personal border patrol. Yours vs mine. Us vs them.

6

On our walks, I tap the top of another hill with the same tiny grey twig each afternoon. Never to maim or cause a moment of grief, but something draws me to visit the colony, knock a gentle hello, watch in astonishment at the triggered call to action. Each small, hard body transforms into a warrior on high alert for the possible predator standing above, while later, at the store, shoppers refuse to follow the directions telling us all which way to go. Refuse to wear masks. Cut in front of the old man grinding beans into coffee. Refuse to keep their distance, a large body collapsing in on itself before scattering about, helpless.

7

Did I try to move the anthill encroaching on our drive in an act of destruction or mercy? The squirming thing we pass by on an evening bike ride and ignore the way, when they keep sharing the same news story, everyone stops noticing. The virus death count, the protesters each night, until illness and protesting become a new way of life. Someone boarded up the downtown bank. Someone put plywood over the boutique windows in case marchers march too hard. The hill still encompassed a marginal size, while everything else grew too unwieldy, so I thought I could move it one foot over, until my shovel slipped in fear of the silence beneath the writhing mass as the tower fell down without a sound, almost like when you mute the TV.

8

In a few weeks, the anthill rebuilt until an afternoon windstorm lifted off their roof to reveal, again, the gaggle of eggs grown now into bigger pearls waiting to be priced, each round bud priceless. Dreaming of eyes, the slow sprout of each leg, as the country slowly wakes, state by state, the mass of tanned bodies stacked on beaches too close, masks covering each face, our faces, until we forget to bend down, forget to examine the mound with too many other things on our minds. Canceled plans to watch the fireworks. Canceled fall trips to pick apples. Canceled pie baking for the county fair ribbon. Canceled winter drives one town over to see the yearly display of gingerbread houses arranged on beds of fake snow, edible neighborhoods where everyone gets their share of dessert without ever having to ask.

9

We ride bikes past the anthill to escape the local news. The virus nips at our heels like the neighborhood dog, fearless against both germs and fast tires. Summer will turn to fall as we pedal past the colony with no plans, now, except to survive the way women once made apple pies with no apples, meatloaf with no meat. In March, we toyed with growing a garden while we watched an ant haul a large green leaf up the hill, but most stores closed, and who mail orders seeds with no soil? Today, it is too hot to consider what happens to ants during winter. In a book, I once read the word "overwinter," which means to huddle around the queen, to survive on your own fat.

Safety in numbers, I think it means.

EVE CONNELL

* **standing still** inaction **the great stall** selfish **challenge** heartbreak **loss** devastation **exhaustion** worst case scenario **pandemic** late-stage capitalism **toxic individualism** apocalypse **failure** inequity **superspreader events** climate emergency **systemic racism** voter suppression **doomscrolling** anti-mask **dumpster fire** shitstorm **wounds** domestic terrorism **food insecurity** gaslighting **contradiction** alternative facts **hoax** isolation **mourning** depletion **threat** tragedy **adversity** police brutality **tyranny** anxiety **entitled** blockade **chaos** division **greed** cruelty **alienation** combative **aggression** cancellation **division** postponement **enemy** meanness **privilege gone awry** zombification **stagnation** insurrection **same as it ever was** refutation **fascism** gasp **destroy** meltdown **abandoned ideals** despair **disinfect** scatter **devalue** annihilate **infect** arrogance **subjugate** disenfranchise **oppress** elimination **detract** stagnant waters **interminable sadness** captivity **soul crushing** belligerent **heedless** cancellation **instability** totalitarianism **nationalistic pageantry** double down **old habits die hard** rant **crisis** fraud **go down with the ship** liability **in harm's way** sever ties **elitism** protectionism **base behavior** struggle **pivot** ease **love** selflessness **humanity** set boundaries **safety zone** asset **phoenix from the ashes** genuine **chance** meditate **new way of being** reframe **grief rites** collectivism **inner strength** plan **observant** noncompliant **heart expanding** freedom **boundless joy** transformation **pollinate** encouragement **nourish** empower **elevate** humility **cultivate** initiation **activate** inhabit **rejuvenate** hope **new dreams** dance it out **replenish** breathe **civil rights** reflect **the new normal** uprising **reimagine** consciousness upgrade **change agents** kindness **allyship** now **mutualism** innovate **protection** nurture **cooperate** compassion

share solidarity **leadership** surrender **gratitude** calm **activism** peaceful protest **opportunity** windfall **security** fulfillment **celebration** companionship **science** truth **confirmation** agency **abundance** scream inside your heart **heal** sunny days ahead **verdant garden** quarantine pods **creative output** freedom **Black Lives Matter** earth in balance **social distancing** justice **success** utopia **independence** thriving community **personal** breakthrough **revitalize** salvation **agency** optimism **acceptance** generous **volition** advocacy **moving forward**

"It's a place straddling normalcy and the abyss. Where you ask yourself, 'How long can this last?' A standstill that highlights the things shifting and changing in our world while allowing us brief moments to appreciate things that never change." —From *The Museum of Purgatory* by Ali Fitzgerald (published in The New Yorker, December 28, 2020)

JANUARY 2021

JANUARY 6 — *INSURRECTION*

JANUARY 20 — *INAUGURATION*

###,### DEATHS | ##,###,### INFECTED

ACKNOWLEDGMENTS

I want to acknowledge every contributor in this book. Thank you.

Among them are personal heroes of mine, dear friends, writers I have published before, and, in some cases, all three of these combined. Plus, several I have only recently met. Either way, I admire each of them for their mind, their talents, and their writing skills.

Special thanks to Amy Chadwick and Eve Connell, your support means everything to me and I love you both.

I acknowledge you too, dear reader, thank you. I hope you feel that this book is a gift, and everyone should read it.

ADRIAN ERNESTO CEPEDA is the author of *Flashes & Verses... Becoming Attractions* from Unsolicited Press, *Between the Spine* from Picture Show Press, and *La Belle Ajar* and *We Are the Ones Possessed* from CLASH Books. His poetry has been featured in *Harvard Palabritas, Glass Poetry: Poets Resist, Cultural Weekly, Yes Poetry, Frontier Poetry, The Fem, poeticdiversity, Rigorous, Luna Luna Magazine, The Wild Word, The Revolution Relaunch,* and *Palette Poetry.* Adrian is an Angelino Poet who lives with his wife and their adorably spoiled cat Woody Gold in Los Angeles, California. [WS: adrianernestocepeda.com | FB: poetnotarockstar | TW: @PoetNotRockStar | IG: thepoetnotarockstar]

Born and raised in Portland, Oregon, **ALEX DANG** started performing poetry at 17 and hasn't slowed down since. He was on the Portland Poetry Slam nationals team, making him the only Asian-American poet in Portland's history to be on the team four years in a row. Alex earned his way to become the Eugene Poetry Grand Slam Champion in 2014, 2015, and again in 2017. He has been a two-time TEDx speaker for University of Oregon and Reno, Nevada. His work has been featured on *Huffington Post, Upworthy,* and *Everyday Feminism,* and has been viewed over 2 million times on YouTube. Alex has performed in over 50 cities, 30 states, 7 countries, and wants to know what your favorite food is. [WS: alexdangpoetry.com | FB: alexdangpoetry | TW: @alexdangpoetry | IG: alexdangpoetry]

ALLY HENNY is a writer and speaker. She holds a B.S. in Psychology from Missouri State University and a Master of Divinity from Fuller Theological Seminary, with an emphasis in Race, Cultural Identity, and Reconciliation. She hopes to pastor a church someday. Ally has been writing about race, identity, culture, and racial conciliation on Twitter, her personal Facebook profile, and on her blog, *The Armchair Commentary*, since 2014. She is Vice President of *The Witness: A Black Christian Collective*, where she also writes about black motherhood and other topics related to the black experience from a faith-based perspective. Ally has participated in several panels and facilitated discussions on America's race issue and has conducted numerous personal education and coaching sessions for individuals seeking to participate in racial conciliation. [WS: allyhenny.com | FB: allyhennypage | TW: @thearmchaircom | IG: allyhenny] [WS: thearmchaircommentary.com | WS: thewitnessbcc.com]

Recognized by Poetry Slam Inc as a "Legend of the South," **AMOJA SUMLER** (author of *Fables, Foibles, & Other 'Merican Sins*) is a nationally celebrated poet, essayist, and one of the preeminent emerging voices of leftist intersectional social advocacy. A Watering Hole graduate fellow and 2020 MFA recipient, Amoja's work throughout the Arkansas poetry scene was a legendary seed. From his essays discussing the role of law enforcement to the value of capitalism, he is best known for fusing the art of the intellectual into the familiar. Amoja has headlined poetry festivals such as the Austin International Poetry Festival, the Bridgewater International Poetry Festival, Write NOLA in New Orleans, and Rock the Republic in Texas. As a resident artist of several southern Arts in Education rosters, Amoja lectures at schools and literary nonprofits, while teaching creative pedagogy and keynoting at social advocacy conferences like Long Beach Indie Film Pedagogy Conference and Furious Flower, throughout the nation. His poetry appears in *The Pierian Literary Journal, Muddy Ford Press, Swimming with Elephants, FreezeRay Poetry*, and *The Antigonish Review* as well as other journals. [FB: momanthepoet | TW: @momanthepoet | IG: momanthepoet]

ASHLEY JAMES has been writing since the third grade when she won an Earth Day poetry competition. She enjoys writing poetry and non-fiction around topics including personal identity, nature/the environment, and various social issues. In addition to this collection, Ashley was recently published in Zora's Den *The Fire Inside* anthology, a collection of stories and poems inspired by Zora Neale Hurston. You can follow Ashley on Instagram through her music page [IG: ashleyamandaacoustic] or her page where she highlights diversity and inclusion outdoors [IG: chasingfalls_].

BEN TANZER is an Emmy Award-winning coach, creative strategist, podcaster, writer, teacher, and social worker who has been helping nonprofits, publishers, authors, small businesses, and career changers tell their stories for 20-plus years. He is the author of the recently re-released short story collection *Upstate*, and several award-winning books, including the science fiction novel *Orphans* and the essay collections *Lost in Space: A Father's Journey There and Back Again* and *Be Cool—a memoir (sort of)*. He is also a lover of all things book, running, gin, and street art. [WS: tanzerben.com | FB: BenTanzer | TW: @BenTanzer | IG: tanzerben]

BRENDAN CANTY is a musician, composer, producer, and filmmaker. Widely known as one of the best drummers of all time, Canty is internationally recognized as a founding member of Fugazi, as well as for his work in bands Deadline, Rites of Spring, Deathfix, Messthetics, and more. Canty has composed soundtracks for television and film, and co-founded the film production companies Trixie, and These Electric Things. He lives in Washington, D.C., with his wife and four children.

BRIAN S. ELLIS is the author of four collections of poetry, the most recent of which is *Often Go Awry* from University of Hell Press. He has been nominated for the Pushcart Prize five times. He lives in Portland, Oregon. [WS: brianellis. info | FB: brian.s.ellis.7 | TW: @roadrunnertwice | IG: brianstephenellis | LI: brian-ellis-362747a]

CHRIS DUPUY is a lifelong sports fan currently residing near the ocean in Southern California. Chris is a regular contributor to *The Big Smoke America*, a former member of the Bay Area Poetry Coalition, and the Founder and Editor in Chief of SportsAttic.blog, a series of essays poking nostalgic fun at the world of sports, with special emphasis on the favorite teams of his youth—the New York Mets, Jets, and Knicks.

CHRIS VALLE is a photographer, musician, (and now, apparently, a writer?) from San Pedro, California by way of St. Louis and San Diego. He's been ranting since Reagan. [WS: chrisvallephoto.com | TW: @TheChrisValle | TW: @chrisvallephoto | IG: chrisvallephoto | IG: chrisvalleqatsi]

CHRISTINE MAUL RICE's novel-in-stories *Swarm Theory* (University of Hell Press) was awarded an Independent Publisher Book Award, a National Indie Excellence Award, a Chicago Writers Association Book of the Year award, and was included in *PANK*'s Best Books of 2016 and Powell's Books Midyear Roundup: The Best Books of 2016 So Far. In 2019, Christine was included in *Newcity Lit*'s "Lit 50: Who Really Books in Chicago 2019" and named one of "30 Writers to Watch" by Chicago's Guild Literary Complex. Christine's short stories and essays have been published in *MAKE: A Literary Magazine, Belt Publishing's Rust Belt Chicago: An Anthology, The Literary Review, The Rumpus, McSweeney's Internet Tendency, The Big Smoke America, The Millions, Chicago Tribune, Detroit Metro Times*, among other publications. Christine is the founder and editor of *Hypertext Magazine*. [WS: christinemaulrice.com | TW: @ChrisMaulRice] [WS: hypertextmag.com]

CORIE SKOLNICK is the author of *ORFAN* and *America's Most Eligible*, hilarious and poignant works of fiction that shine an often hilarious light on familial relationships and the human condition. Hailing from Chicago, Illinois, where she grew up during the Civil Rights Movement, Corie now lives in San Diego, California. Her novels are often informed by her more than two decades as a marriage and family therapist and a professor of psychology focusing on early childhood development and clinical applications of psychology in human relationships. Find links to her other work in Desto3.

com, *The Big Smoke America, NAILED Magazine, Muse, Adoption Reunion in the Social Media Age,* and *Adoption Therapy.* Corie is the co-founder of WE TALK, a social connections project (leaplearnlive.org/we-talk.html) of the national educational non-profit organization Leap Learn Live, serving single mothers across America. [WS: corieskolnick.com | FB: corieskolnick | TW: @corieskolnick | IG: corieskolnick]

DANG NGUYEN is a father and a fisherman. I used to own Bar Pink (thanks, COVID!) and I now run a small record label (again, thanks, COVID!). I am a non-profit director, and a for-profit collector. I am a refugee, and I would eat that. [TW: @skipperdang | IG: skipperdang | IG: pink_pachyderm_records]

DeMISTY D. BELLINGER lives and teaches in Massachusetts. She is the author of the poetry collections *Rubbing Elbows* (Finishing Line Press) and *Peculiar Heritage* (Mason Jar Press), and the forthcoming novel *New to Liberty* (Unnamed Press). DeMisty is a poetry editor with Porcupine Literary and with Malarkey Books. [WS: demistybellinger.com | TW: @DeMistyB]

Though **DIAN GREENWOOD** started in the Dakotas, she has been a "west coaster" since adolescence. She studied both writing and counseling psychology in San Francisco. An early focus on poetry led her to fiction. She has personal essays published in *The Big Smoke America*. She writes and works as a therapist in Portland, Oregon. [FB: dian.greenwood]

ELLEN YAFFA tiptoed into flash narrative in 2008 and has been hooked on short form writing ever since. She is an active and enthusiastic member of "Thursday Writers," a program of San Diego Writers, Ink, and an alumna of several writing workshops emphasizing flash narrative and short shorts. Her work has been published in *Dime Stories* and *Thursday Writers Anthologies*, as well as *A Year in Ink* and *The Sun Magazine*. Ellen also creates multi-media art journals. *Through My Eyes*, her first book, is a collection of flash narratives and original collages, and is available through Amazon.

ERIC WITCHEY has sold stories under several names, in twelve genres, and on six continents. He has received awards or recognition from New Century Writers, Writers of the Future, Writer's Digest, Independent Publisher Book Awards, International Book Awards, The Eric Hoffer Prose Award Program, Short Story America, the Irish Aeon Awards, and other organizations. His How-To articles have appeared in *The Writer Magazine, Writer's Digest Magazine*, and other print and online magazines. He currently teaches the Fiction Fluency creative writing program for WordCrafters, a 501(c)3 non-profit literary organization: https://wordcrafters.org/fiction-fluency-pricing-registration/ [WS: ericwitchey.com | TW: @EWitchey | IG: ericm.witchey | Shared Blog: shadowspinners.wordpress.com]

EVE CONNELL is a Brand Driver and Consummate Connector. Her main activities? Empowering people through resources sharing, skills building, and constant cheerleading efforts. Editing all sorts of stuff so folks shine. Working for good, not evil, by engaging in social justice, racial equity, and climate action initiatives. Also: there's more. [WS: eveconnell.com | TW: @mizconnell | IG: mizconnell] [WS: artzeronow.com | TW: @artzeronow | IG: art.zero.now]

FLORENCIA ORLANDONI spends most of her time facilitating discussion-based writing courses and teaching Spanish. When she is not teaching, she reads nonfiction and writes on the subjects of feminism and immigration in Latin America. Florencia strives to be a writer who approaches topics with an informed mind, an honest spirit, a compassionate heart, and a good sense of humor. Though she was born and raised in Argentina, she currently resides in Los Angeles with her husband, father, two brothers, two cats, two dogs, five goats, and 26 chickens. [TW: @FloriOrlandoni]

GABINO IGLESIAS is a writer, editor, and literary critic living in Austin. He is the author of *Zero Saints* and *Coyote Songs*. He has been nominated to the Bram Stoker Award twice, the Locus Award, and won the Wonderland Book Award for Best Novel in 2019. He teaches creative writing at SNHU's online MFA program. [TW: @Gabino_Iglesias]

ISOBEL O'HARE is a poet, erasure artist, essayist, and memoirist-in-progress based in Roanoke, Virginia. They are the author of *all this can be yours* and editor of *Erase the Patriarchy: An Anthology of Erasure Poetry*, both available from University of Hell Press. Isobel earned an MFA in Writing from Vermont College of Fine Arts and they are a Helene Wurlitzer Foundation fellow. Isobel is the founding editor of the magazine and small press Dream Pop. [WS: isobelohare.com]

JACKIE SHANNON HOLLIS is the author of the memoir, *This Particular Happiness: A Childless Love Story* (Forest Avenue Press). During *2020, in addition to getting that puppy, she has been trying her hand at the baritone ukulele, songwriting, and becoming comfortable with her own voice making notes. She and her husband Bill spend plenty of time in the garden, where she grows the veggies and flowers and he does the heavy lifting and builds art that surprises her. Jackie's short stories and essays have appeared in a variety of publications. Her novel, *At the Wheat Line*, is a work in progress. [WS: jackieshannonhollis.com | FB: Jackie.Shannon.Hollis | TW: @JShannonHollis | IG: jackie.shannon.hollis]

JAMES JAY EDWARDS is a member of the San Diego Film Critics Society and the Online Film Critics Society. His work can be read at *The Big Smoke America* (thebigsmoke.com) and heard on the Eye on Horror podcast (eyeonhorror. buzzsprout.com). He lives in San Diego with his wife, two (other) dogs, and cat. [TW: @CinemaFearite]

JASON ARMENT served in Operation Iraqi Freedom as a Machine Gunner in the USMC. He's earned an MFA in Creative Nonfiction from the Vermont College of Fine Arts. His work has appeared in *The Iowa Review, The Rumpus, ESPN, The Best American Essays 2017,* and *The New York Times,* among other publications. His memoir about the war in Iraq, *Musalaheen* (University of Hell Press), stands in stark contrast to other narratives about Iraq in both content and quality. Jason lives and works in Denver. [WS: jasonarment.com]

JASON ZENOBIA is a trained, professional chef, an incompetent juggler, and has run out of space for any new tattoos. He writes, is a commercial voice-over actor, and is an audiobook narrator/producer living and working in Portland, Oregon with his husband of 27 years and a dwindling supply of cats. He is a fan of Cartoons, Whiskey, and Billie Holiday. [WS: zenobiavoice.com]

JENNY FORRESTER has been published in *Nailed Magazine, pompom lit, Seattle's City Arts, Gobshite Quarterly, GetSparked, One Typed Page, Portland Review, Indiana Review, Columbia Review,* and Seattle's *City Arts Magazine.* She's been anthologized in *Places Like Home* and *Magical Writing,* published by Ariel Gore, and in *Listen to Your Mother,* Putnam. She's published dozens of emerging and established writers in the Unchaste Anthologies, curates the Unchaste Variety Show on her own and in collaboration with Death Rattle Writers in Idaho and with Zines & Things, and hosts Creatives Study Hall. She's been interviewed by Wyoming Public Radio, *The Colorado Sun,* and has been reviewed by *High Country News.* She's the author of *Narrow River, Wide Sky: A Memoir* and *Soft Hearted Stories: Seeking Saviors, Cowboy Stylists, and Other Fallacies of Authoritarianism,* a Colorado Book Award Finalist, 2020. She seeks connection through jennyforrester.com, unchastereaders.com, and various other social media platforms in order to dismantle the Anthropocene. [WS: jennyforrester.com | FB: jenny.forrester.507 | TW: @jennyforrester8 | IG: jennyforresterauthor] [WS: unchastereaders.com]

JOE AUSTIN is a swiftly-aging mid-50s father of three, who spends his free time complaining and/or clawing for some shred of remaining relevance. The reopening of his bar, the Live Wire, after COVID has buoyed his spirits greatly, but he's still very much an acquired taste. [TW: @joeaustin247 | IG: joeaustin247] [WS: livewirebar.bigcartel.com | FB: livewirebar | TW: @livewirebar | IG: livewirebar]

JOHN S. BLAKE was born and raised on the lower east side of Manhattan and now resides in Albuquerque, New Mexico. Blake is a VCU Grad, MFA student at Sierra Nevada University, Watering Hole Graduate Fellow, TEDx speaker, essayist for *The Big Smoke America*, spoken word artist, as well as a literacy tutor, lecturer, and mentor. Blake facilitates workshops, lectures, and performs nationwide: universities, high schools, middle schools, detention centers, prisons, and youth programs. He has been nominated for a Pushcart Prize and published in *Naugatuck River Review of Narrative Poetry, ARDOR Literary Magazine, 2 Bridges Review, Criminal Class Press, Beyond Race Magazine, Sparrow Ghost Anthology, In The Fray, Pen-It! Magazine, Malpais Review, Adobe Walls, Red Fez*, and *TrackAhead*. He's been interviewed for PBS and radio programs. His studies focus on gender/sexuality and a concentration in toxic masculinity and intersectional praxis to dismantle patriarchal ideology in young men in order to be instrumental in changing society's views on the subjects of race and gender, sexuality and class. Blake also works with recovering addicts in order to help them navigate sobriety through reflexive essays and group discussions in order to alleviate shame and map healthier coping mechanisms in recovery. [WS: johnsblake.com | FB: JohnSBlakePoet | TW: @ BlackFluidPoet | IG: blackfluidpoet | TikTok: blackfluidpoet]

JOSEPH EDWIN HAEGER is the author of the experimental memoir *Learn to Swim* (University of Hell Press). His writing has appeared at *Vol. 1 Brooklyn, Drunk Monkeys, X-R-A-Y, HAD*, and others. As a litmus test, he likes to tell people his favorite movie is *Face/Off*, but a part of him is afraid it's true. He lives in the PNW. [TW: @JoeTurquoise | IG: RoyalSwine]

KATE RISTAU is the author of the middle grade series, *Clockbreakers*, and the young adult series, *Shadow Girl*. You can read her essays in *The New York Times* and *The Washington Post*. In her ideal world, magic and myth combine to create memorable stories with unforgettable characters. Until she finds that world, she'll live in a house in Oregon, where they found a sword behind the water heater and fairies in the backyard. [WS: kateristau.com | FB: kateristau | TW: @kateristau | IG: kateristau]

KENNING JP GARCÍA is an antipoet and diarist. Xe is the author of the notvel, *OF (What Place Meant)* (West Vine Press) as well as the speculative epic ebooks, *ROBOT* and *Yawning on the Sands*. [IG: kenyjpgarcia]

KIMBERLY SHERIDAN is a nonfiction writer and Fascial Stretch Therapist. She holds an MFA in creative nonfiction from Eastern Washington University where she served as the managing editor of *Willow Springs* magazine. [WS: kimberlysheridanwrites.com | IG: drawonthewalls]

LAUREN GILMORE is an incoming MA student in Lehigh University's Literature and Social Justice program. Her short fiction/poetry has appeared in *Hayden's Ferry Review*, *Ghost City Review*, *Rogue Agent*, and other journals, and she has contributed to *Horror Homeroom* and *The Pacific Northwest Inlander*. Her full-length collection of poetry, *Outdancing the Universe*, is available from University of Hell Press. [WS: laurengilmore.com | TW: @laurnsaurus]

LEAH NOBLE DAVIDSON's work addresses how we understand our world through experiments with our language frames. She has two bestselling books through University of Hell Press: *Poetic Scientifica*, a one-poem book with a 120-page glossary, and *DOOR*, a tunneling book about one word. Leah has spent months touring the US with her poetry and has been featured in a number of publications. She's been nominated for and has won some writing awards with fancy names. She lives in Portland, Oregon. Her house has just enough light on the front porch. [WS: lnobledavidson.com | TW: @askrofquestions | IG: poetscientifica | LI: lndavidson]

LEYNA RYNEARSON is a poet and math tutor living in Portland, Oregon. They have spent the pandemic hanging out with their cats, plants, husband, and roommate's dog; expanding their knowledge of data analysis tools; and exploring watercolor. You can find their watercolors and art-based musings on Instagram at @superleyna and you can find their normal animal-, mineral-, and vegetable-based musings on Instagram at @leynarae. [IG: superleyna | IG: leynarae]

LINDA RAND is an Art Witch and Wolf Mama living in Portland, Oregon. She has been published in *Entropy, Nailed Magazine, Unchaste Anthology Volume I*, as well as anthologies *Places Like Home, City of Weird,* and *The People's Apocalypse*, with non-fiction journal excerpts in *Fuck Happiness: How Women Are Ditching the Cult of Positivity and Choosing Radical Joy* by Ariel Gore. Her artwork has been included in *PDX Magazine* and the book *Oneira: I Dream the Self.* [WS: etsy.com/shop/BirdsWayBotanicals | IG: lindapaintsandwrites]

LIZ SCOTT is a clinical psychologist and writer who lives and works in Portland, Oregon. Her memoir, *This Never Happened*, was published by University of Hell Press. [WS: lizscott.org | FB: elizabeth.scott.39395 | TW: @lizscottpdx | IG: lizscottpdx]

NANCY TOWNSLEY is a longtime community newspaper journalist living in a floating home on the Multnomah Channel near Portland, Oregon. Her work has appeared in *The Timberline Review* (Winter/Spring 2018), *NAILED Magazine, Elephant Journal, The Big Smoke America*, and *Brave on the Page: Oregon Writers on Craft and the Creative Life* (Forest Avenue Press). She is working on a novel about a journalist-turned-activist in a time of devalued news. [WS: nancytownsley.com | IG: nancy.townsley]

RABB ASAD lives in Atlanta, Georgia, and earned his MFA from Bennington College. Rabb also holds degrees from Sarah Lawrence College and Harvard University.

RASHAUN J. ALLEN is an Instructor of English at Westchester Community College and the author of several independently published poetry collections, including *The Blues Cry For A Revolution*, which was an Amazon Kindle Best Seller in African American Poetry. [WS: rashaunjallen.com | TW: @rashaunjallen]

RAN WALKER is the author of twenty-three books, the latest of which is *Keep It*

100: 100-Word Stories. He is the winner of the Indie Author Project's inaugural Indie Author of the Year and the Black Caucus of the American Library Association Fiction Ebook Award. He teaches creative writing at Hampton University and lives with his wife and daughter in Virginia. [WS: ranwalker. com | TW: @ranwalker]

SEAN DAVIS is the author of *The Wax Bullet War, Oregon Wildland Firefighting: A History*, and *The Jesus He Deserved*. He has an MFA from Pacific University, and he lives on the McKenzie River in rural Oregon with his wife, daughters, and two giant dogs. [WS: seandaviswriter.com FB: SeanDavisWriter | TW: @OriginalSeanD | IG: sean_davis___]

SHANNON BRAZIL is a genre-fluid writer and performer whose prose appears in *Hip Mama, 580-Split, NAILED Magazine*, and elsewhere. She's the recipient of a Literary Arts Award for Drama. "My piece is dedicated to Mary Kushner, gone too soon, who did everything she could to keep me sane and keep me writing for nearly twenty years. Thank you to University of Hell Press for giving my weird, broken art a place to live." [FB: Shannon.brazil | TW: @ShanBrazil | IG: shannonbrazilpdx]

SKYLER REED (Paiute / Klamath Tribes) is a Folklife Slam Champion, awardee of the University of Washington iSchool's Dean's Fellowship for Library Science, and the founder of Moved By Words, a platform dedicated to finding and sharing new voices in writing communities. Skyler's currently working on building a network of archivists to distribute indigenous knowledge. [WS: movedbywords.org | EM: skyler@movedbywords.org]

STACEY Y. CLARK is the founder and Executive Director of Leap Learn Live (L3), a 501(c)(3) nonprofit based in Fort Worth, Texas. L3 provides at-risk single mothers everywhere with free, wellness-based life skills, and lifestyle, training, and coaching. Stacey believes in the power of building relationships and is the developer and co-organizer of "We Talk," a national, intercultural, personal diversity and inclusion program for women. Stacey has over 20 years of communications and learning and development experience, a master's degree in education, and a PhD, in overcoming adversity. [WS: leaplearnlive.org]

Before the pandemic, **SUZANNE BURNS** had never observed an anthill, or anything in nature. Out of work from March 16th to July 8th of 2020, she and her husband looked forward to visiting the neighborhood anthills as much as they once looked forward to travel.

TIM MAYS was born in the '50s in Hollywood, California. After his parents divorced, he grew up in Barstow, and then he moved to San Diego in 1972 to attend SDSU. Tim started promoting punk rock concerts in 1980, opened Pink Panther in 1986 (lost lease in 1990), Casbah in 1989 (which then moved to its current location in 1994), Turf Supper Club in 1998 (subsequently forced out by a greedy landlord in 2008), Krakatoa in 2004, Starlite in 2007, Vinyl Junkies Record Shack in 2017, and became part owner of Soda Bar in 2017. The Casbah now promotes concerts in-house 360 days a year, as well as shows at Soda Bar, Belly Up, Music Box, Observatory North Park, House of Blues, Soma, Spreckels Theatre, and more. [FB: tim.mays.52 | IG: mrmazee] [WS: casbahmusic.com | WS: krakatoacafe.com | WS: vinyljunkies.net | WS: starlitesandiego.com | WS: sodabarmusic.com]

TRACY BURKHOLDER is the author of *All Land an Island. All Blue the Sea*, a collection of photo/freewrites, and *I Want More*, a hybrid of lyric memoir, poetry, and image. Her writing has also appeared in numerous journals including *The Cincinnati Review, PANK*, and *Vinyl*. She can be found online at tracyburkholder.com and on Instagram @t.a.burkholder while she herself can be found in Portland, Oregon. [WS: tracyburkholder.com | IG: t.a.burkholder]

TRAVIS LAURENCE NAUGHT is an author who happens to be a quadriplegic wheelchair user. *The Virgin Journals* (ASD Publishing), a paperback volume of his poetry, and *Joyride* (Black Rose Writing), a novel, are both available through online retailers. Travis received an undergraduate degree in psychology and completed coursework toward a graduate degree in sports psychology from Eastern Washington University. [WS: naughtapoet.blogspot.com | FB: travis. naught | IG: travislaurencenaught | YT: Travis Naught]

WRYLY T. McCUTCHEN is a hybrid writer, interdisciplinary performer, teaching artist, & 2018 LAMBDA Fellow. Their poetry has appeared in *Foglifter, Papeachu Review,* & *Nat. Brut.* Wryly holds a dual genre MFA in creative nonfiction & poetry from Antioch University Los Angeles & teaches writing at Hugo House. Their debut collection, *My Ugly and Other Love Snarls*, was published in 2017 by University of Hell Press. Wryly resides on unceded lands, stewarded by the Cowlitz & Clackamas peoples, where they cast spells in text & flesh & sweat. [IG: wryly_xder | Venmo: Wryly-McCutchen]

ZAJI COX has been creating stories since she started reading at age three. She discovered her passion for writing when she wrote her first short story at nine years old, self-publishing a book of fiction at thirteen, and a compilation of short stories in 2016. She has been invited to participate at several literary events in Portland including the PDX Poetry Festival, Survival of the Feminist reading series, Corporeal Writing's LOOP, and more. In early 2020, she was the winner in the poetry category of Submission PDX's reading series. She holds a BA in English, and her writing can be found in *Cultural Weekly, Pathos* Literary Magazine, *Entropy Magazine*, and others. [WS: zaji.journoportfolio.com | IG: zajitheartist] [WS: patreon.com/zajitheartist]

GREG GERDING is a noted underground poet and publisher. He graduated from the University of Maryland with a BA in English Language and Literature, and then hit the streets to continue his education as a scholar and scrivener of the real world. He is the author of seven books: five books of prose poetry (*Poetry in Hell, The Burning Album of Lame, Loser Makes Good, Piss Artist,* and *The Idiot Parade*), a collection of short nonfiction stories about the bars of San Diego (*Venue Voyeurisms*), and an oral history on the subject of intimacy (*I'll Show You Mine*), plus several chapbooks.

Greg started his writing career, quite literally, in Hell. In 1994, he conceived and hosted a weekly open mic art series—Poetry in Hell—in a Washington, D.C., basement bar called Hell showcasing poetry, prose, music, comedy, and performance art. Hell then followed Greg in 1996 to San Diego, California, where he quickly became a major fixture in the literary scene. He wrote two weekly columns, *Venue Voyeurism* and *University of Hell*, for *The Weekly San Diego* from 1999 to 2000.

Greg founded University of Hell Press in 2005 as a self-publishing brand while in San Diego. He then moved to Portland, Oregon, in 2008. In 2012, he expanded the brand and started publishing others, providing a platform for unconventional artistry and ferreting out unique artists everywhere. The press is deliberately genre-less, flexible, and open to publishing important works that might not otherwise see the light of day.

Greg is also Editor-in-Chief of *The Big Smoke America*, a leading opinions and editorials site. *The Big Smoke* was first launched in Australia by Founder and CEO Alexandra Tselios in 2013 and it quickly permeated the mainstream media as a dynamic voice in a stale media landscape. Alexandra, with plans to spread *The Big Smoke* across multiple countries, tapped Greg to launch *The Big Smoke America* in 2015. He has published essays and articles on important, wide-ranging topics every day since then.

Greg was born in Kentucky, has lived and/or worked in nearly every city in America, and currently resides in Portland, Oregon.

by Rory Douglas
The Most Fun You'll Have at a Cage Fight

by Brian S. Ellis
American Dust Revisited
Often Go Awry

by Greg Gerding
The Burning Album of Lame
Venue Voyeurisms: Bars of San Diego
Loser Makes Good: Selected Poems 1994
Piss Artist: Selected Poems 1995-1999
The Idiot Parade: Selected Poems 2000-2005

by Lauren Gilmore
Outdancing the Universe

by Rob Gray
The Immaculate Collection / The Rhododendron and Camellia Year Book (1966)

by Joseph Edwin Haeger
Learn to Swim

by Lindsey Kugler
HERE.

by Shawn Levy
A Year in the Life of Death

by Wryly T. McCutchen
My Ugly & Other Love Snarls

by Michael McLaughlin
Countless Cinemas

by Johnny No Bueno
We Were Warriors
Concrete & Juniper

by Isobel O'Hare
all this can be yours (hardcover & paperback)

by A.M. O'Malley
Expecting Something Else

by Stephen M. Park
High & Dry
The Grass Is Greener

by Christine Rice
Swarm Theory

by Thomas Lucky Richards
Thirst for Beginners: Poems, Prose, and Quizzes

by Liz Scott
This Never Happened

by Michael N. Thompson
A Murder of Crows

by Ellyn Touchette
The Great Right-Here

by Ran Walker
Most of My Heroes Don't Appear on No Stamps

by Sarah Xerta
Nothing to Do with Me